# EPILOGUES AND PRAYERS

*also by William Barclay*

CRUCIFIED AND CROWNED

THE GOSPELS AND ACTS

JESUS AS THEY SAW HIM

MANY WITNESSES, ONE LORD

THE MASTER'S MEN

THE MIND OF JESUS

A NEW PEOPLE'S LIFE OF JESUS

NEW TESTAMENT WORDS

PRAYERS FOR THE CHRISTIAN YEAR

WILLIAM BARCLAY

# Epilogues and Prayers

SCM PRESS LTD

To
the members of
the Youth Fellowship of
Trinity Church of Scotland, Renfrew
1933-1946
who taught me far more
than I taught them

334 00378 4

First published 1963
by SCM Press Ltd
26–30 Tottenham Road, London N1
Eleventh impression 1982

Printed in Great Britain by
Richard Clay (The Chaucer Press) Ltd
Bungay, Suffolk

# CONTENTS

6

7

# FOREWORD

MOST of the Epilogues in this book have already appeared in the pages of the *British Weekly*. I am most grateful to Rev. Denis Duncan, BD, the editor of that newspaper, for permission to publish them in this more permanent form. It is my hope that Youth Leaders and Club Leaders and all who have to lead worship with young people will find them of some use in their work, than which none could be more important.

I am as ever grateful for the help and the advice of Rev. David L. Edwards, the editor of the SCM Press, and for the care and attention of his staff in the production of this book.

WILLIAM BARCLAY

*Trinity College,*
*Glasgow*

# WORSHIP WITH YOUNG PEOPLE

THE Epilogue is one particular form of the public worship of God. It must therefore be looked at not in isolation but in the context of worship as a whole. We must therefore begin by asking what we are trying to do when we lead the worship of a group or of a congregation.

The widest possible answer to that question is that *we are seeking to make people aware of the presence of God*. We are not asking God to be with us, for there is no time when God is not with us. We are not trying to lead people into the presence of God, for there is no time when they are not in the presence of God. Sometimes in leading worship and in introducing prayer we find ourselves saying: 'Let us ask for the presence of God with us.' That is to ask for something which we already have. What we are really trying to do in worship is to make them aware of the presence of God, to make them realize the presence of God, and to make them certain that the God who is there is there to receive and to help.

But there is clearly something to be added to this. To be aware of the presence of God depends for its value entirely on our conception of the God of whose presence we are aware. If we can think of God only, as Hardy put it, as 'the dreaming, dark, dumb thing that turns the handle of the idle show', there is not much value in being aware of his presence. If we can think of God as no more than cynically amused at the antics of the creatures he has made, there is not much value in being aware of his presence. If we can think of God only as avenging justice, or only as outraged majesty, there is not much value in being aware of his presence. If we can think of God only as the Greek philosophers thought of him, if we can think of him only as wrapped in an infinite serenity, the condition of which is that he is essentially insulated against all feeling, there is not much value in being aware of his presence. If the awareness of the presence of God is to have any value at all, we must think of God in certain terms.

9

We must believe, if we may put it so, in the *availability* of God. We must believe that God does care and that God does hear and that God does answer. It is an embarrassing thing to visit a house where one is far from sure of a welcome; it is a humiliating thing to visit a house, and to know that someone is in, and to find that the door is deliberately unopened. There would be no point in seeking to make oneself aware of the presence of a God who was deliberately deaf, and who did not wish to be disturbed by men.

This is simply to say that we must believe in the *love* of God. No child would ever think of going to a loveless parent with a request. No one would ever go for help to a man who was known to be hard and unsympathetic and mean. There would be no point in going to a God who does not care. The very presupposition of prayer is the love of God.

We must believe in the *wisdom* of God. It is perfectly true that prayer should be a thing of all times and of all conditions; but the fact remains that it is in times when we are at our wit's end, in times when life is bewildering and perplexing and agonizing, in times when we stand at some cross-roads and do not know which way to take, in times when we are acutely aware that we can neither bear the burdens of life or face the temptations of life, that prayer becomes most intense. Life is full of times when we unload our worries on the man who knows. In time of illness the arrival of the doctor, especially if he is loved and trusted, at once brings relief, for the man who knows is in charge. Even in so mundane a thing as trouble with a motor car or a television set, we simply take our troubles to the man who knows, and leave him to sort them out. There would be little point in prayer to a God who is as limited as ourselves. We must believe in the wisdom of God to give and to guide as we need.

We must believe in the *power* of God. It is precisely man's own helplessness which moves him to pray. There have been thinkers who have thought of God as a struggling God, as a God who himself was wrestling with opposing forces with the issue in the balance. But there would be little point in prayer to a God who is as helpless to deal with life as ourselves.

Israel Abrahams writes nobly of the Jewish view of prayer in the Second Series of *Studies in Pharisaism and the Gospels*. 'Prayer,' he says, 'becomes a harmony between the human and

10

the divine. It is the divine in man going out to meet the divine in God; it is the upward rise of the soul to its heavenly fount. A praying man, as the Pharisees said, is in the divine presence . . . It lays the heart of man on the altar of God.' 'God wants the heart,' is another Jewish saying on prayer.

This is great—but how much greater must prayer be for the Christian, who really knows what his faith means? Prayer is becoming aware of God; but the God of whom we seek to become aware is the God whom we know in terms of Jesus Christ. It is all very well to speak of God as pure spirit, as ultimate being, as final reality; it is all very well to speak of God as a mathematician, as a great astronomer did. But the fact remains that the ordinary person—and perhaps even the philosopher too—cannot pray to an abstraction. The God to whom we pray has the face of Jesus of Nazareth. That is why we can be certain of his availability, of his love, of his wisdom, and of his power.

What we have been saying is applicable to any act of prayer; these are principles which are universally valid. Now we have to bring them to the Epilogue in particular which is our concern. What steps are we to take to try to bring this awareness of God to the members of the group?

(i) First and foremost, there is the necessity of the most careful, meticulous and detailed preparation. It is always wrong to offer to God that which cost us nothing (II Sam. 24.24), and never more so than in an act of worship. This preparation must be on two levels.

There must be the most careful *practical* preparation. There is nothing more intangible and indefinable than what we call atmosphere. There is nothing harder to create and nothing easier to destroy. The practical details of the Epilogue must be arranged far ahead. To be flicking through the pages of the Bible looking at the last minute for a passage to read, to be consulting with the organist or the pianist at the last minute for a hymn to sing, is the sure way to wreck effectiveness. For the pianist to be turning over the pages of the hymn-book either during the reading of the lesson, or worse, during the prayer is a serious distraction. Anything that savours of fuss or last-minute preparation must be carefully avoided.

There must be the most careful *spiritual* preparation. Here must be laid down the first of all rules which he who leads

11

public worship must always remember. *It is not his own prayers that he is bringing to God; it is the prayers of the group.*

There are few worse faults in the leading of public prayer than subjectivism. If the leader thinks only in terms of himself and of his own feelings, then the group will be at the mercy of his mood. If he is depressed, he will produce a cry from the depths, while many may have come to worship in the joy of life. If it so happens that he is happy, he may have all sun-light and nothing for those for whom the light has gone out. If he is obsessed with the thought and the consciousness of sin, he may completely forget those who are radiant with the assurance of salvation.

This kind of preparation means far more than the mere sitting down to prepare an Epilogue. It means that the leader must sit down and visualize his group; he must think his way into their hearts and minds, until he feels with their emotions and thinks with their thoughts. That means that he must know them and equally that he must love them. It is difficult, if not impossible, to see how any preacher or teacher or leader can adequately prepare prayers for the public worship of his congregation or class or group without incessant and faithful pastoral visitation. He must know their joys and their sorrows; their triumphs and their failures; their successes and their disappointments; their temptations and their interests; their work and their pleasure. This is the kind of preparation which will turn a formality into something warm and quivering with life. Detached preparation may produce something which is liturgically perfect; but only this preparation which involves itself in the life situation of the group can produce that which will really lift the heart to God and bring its needs to the divine pity and power. This is not to say that there is no place left for impromptu and extempore prayer; that too has its place. But it is to say that the main lines of the prayer, the needs of the people to be remembered, must be carefully thought out and prepared.

The preparation should not only be mental preparation; the material should be written out in full. The human memory is notoriously fallible, and, if that is not done, there will be times when the leader will have the humiliating and hurting experience of finding that in his prayer he has omitted the need of

12

the very person who needed prayer most. It is characteristic of the Spirit that the Spirit gives his help most richly to those who are prepared to work the hardest. The most careful preparation so far from being a denial of the Spirit is the means of opening the widest door to the help of the Spirit.

(ii) We must now think of the actual material which we are going to use in prayer, how it is to be arranged, and of what it is to consist, and how it is to be expressed.

(a) In the leading of public prayer the leader should always be *orderly* in the arrangement of his material. A prayer which jumps from one subject to another is inevitably difficult to follow; he who listens never knows where he is and never knows what will come next; and the inevitable result is that his attention wanders; he abandons the attempt to follow it; and he therefore ceases to share in it. There is a pattern of prayer and that pattern should be followed. In that pattern there are six different parts.

1. There is *invocation*. Invocation literally means a calling upon God. It is with this that an act of worship opens. As we have already said, it is not that we call upon God to be present with us, for he is always present, but rather that we ask him to enable us to approach him and to make us aware of his presence.

2. There is *confession*. In this we tell God of our sins and our mistakes and we ask for his forgiveness for them.

3. There is *thanksgiving*. In this we thank God for his gifts and ask him to make us mindful of, and grateful, for them.

4. There is *petition*. In this we take our needs to God and ask him for all the gifts we need to enable us to live life more nearly as we ought.

5. There is *intercession*. In this we take to God the needs of others, asking him to bless them. We should be careful always to remember the duty of intercession, for to remember it keeps us from being selfish in our prayers.

6. There is the *blessing*. One point is to be remembered about the blessing. The blessing may be used with the word *you* or the word *us*. For example, we may say: 'The grace of the Lord Jesus Christ be with *us* all,' or we may say, 'The grace of the Lord Jesus Christ be with *you* all.' The first form is really a prayer, and the second form is really a blessing.

13

This means that only in the second form, only in the blessing form, should the hand and arm be raised, for that is only appropriate in a blessing, and not in a prayer.

In a full service all six parts of the pattern of prayer will have their place in the pattern. In the Epilogue it is seldom possible to include them all, but the leader should see to it that over a period each part of the pattern receives its due place.

It is often helpful to introduce each part of the pattern of prayer with a bidding phrase. For instance, we can introduce the thanksgiving by saying: 'Let us now give thanks to God for all his gifts,' or the intercession by saying: 'Let us now ask God to bless others,' and so on. The use of this is that it tells the group just what the leader is going to do and prepares them to share in it.

Before we leave the pattern of prayer, it is well to remember the place of *silence* in prayer. One of the most serious errors in prayer is to think of prayer altogether in terms of *speaking* to God; prayer is just as much *listening* to God. Prayer is at least as much God telling us as it is us telling God. And unless there is silence in prayer we do not give ourselves the opportunity to listen to the voice of God. And, in addition to that, it has always to be remembered that it is not possible in any prayer to bring to God everyone's thanksgiving, everyone's confession, everyone's needs, everyone's friends and dear ones. It is therefore good to have a period of brief silence in every part of the pattern. At the end of each part of the pattern the leader may say, for example, 'Let us be silent and in the silence let each one of us bring his own special thanksgiving to God,' or 'Let us be silent and let us each ask God's forgiveness for anything of which now we are ashamed.' Prayer is at least as much in need of silence as it is of words.

(b) In public prayer the leader must always aim to make his prayers *intelligible*. As in the case of preparation, there are two levels in this matter of intelligibility.

1. There is the matter of *language*. No one will really listen to what he does not understand; and even if by chance a man does listen, quite certainly his thoughts will soon be elsewhere and his mind will be thinking of something else. The disaster of religious language is that it is almost true to say that there are many ordinary people who do not expect it to yield any

14

intelligible sense; they are so used to the fact that it means nothing to them that they have consciously or unconsciously given up expecting it to mean everything.

Sometimes, for instance, we will hear a leader pray entirely in language that is taken from the Psalms; his whole prayer is a mosaic of the language of the devotion of Israel. Sometimes a leader will use biblical phrases which have long since become unintelligible to the layman and to the non-student. A man may begin a prayer: 'O Lord Jesus, who art the alpha and the omega,' and it is by no means everyone who knows that *alpha* and *omega* are the first and last letters of the Greek alphabet, and even if he did know, he might well be puzzled to know why Jesus Christ is addressed in terms of the Greek alphabet. Or, a leader may begin: 'O Lord God, who art throned amid the cherubim and seraphim,' and it is by no means everyone who knows that cherubim and seraphim are kinds of angels in the Jewish angelic hierarchy, and that in fact they are plurals, for in Hebrew the suffix *-im* is the plural ending of masculine nouns. This kind of example could be multiplied endlessly.

There are certain things that we do well to remember. First and foremost, we are not aiming at dignity; we are aiming at reality. We are not primarily aiming at literary beauty; we are aiming to be meaningful. We are not aiming at producing musical and sonorous phrases; we are trying to take the needs and desires of ordinary people and to lay them before God. Further, it is to be remembered that the language of the New Testament itself is very simple. It is far from being elaborate or even beautiful Greek; it is often ungrammatical, often colloquial, just the kind of Greek that people spoke to each other in the street every day. It is the same kind of language that we ought to use when we pray. There is no point in asking God to *vouchsafe* us something, when we might just as well ask him to *give* it to us, and in *beseeching* him to do something when we might just as well *ask* him to do so.

It has always seemed to me that the word by which Jesus called God, and the word by which he taught us to call God settles this matter. That word is *Abba* (Mark 14.36; Rom. 8.15; Gal. 4.6). That word *Abba* was the word by which a Jewish child called his father in the home circle. If it occurred in secular Hebrew, it would quite certainly be translated 'Daddy'.

15

Now, of course, we cannot translate it that way; to do so would be grotesque. But what the word does do is to indicate and summarize a whole attitude to God; and that attitude and relationship is one of the closest intimacy. We go to God as we would go to an earthly father whom we love and trust. And quite certainly on such an occasion no one in his senses would talk to his father in Elizabethan English which no man has used for almost four centuries. Such language has a double disadvantage. It makes prayer language unnatural to the ordinary person. And it almost unconsciously includes prayer with things archaic like Gothic architecture and stained-glass windows. Why should the language of devotion have stood still for ever in the Book of Psalms? Why should the language of the Christian man have come to a halt for ever in the reign of King James the Sixth? Cannot a man speak to God, not in the slang, and not in the colloquialism, but in the best language which his own day and generation can provide? Surely in his prayers a man is better to speak to God in his own language than in what is now a synthetic and archaic amalgam of a speech that is long since dead, as far as the lips of men are concerned.

Very often this comes to its peak in the vexed question of whether we are to address God as *Thou* or *You*. If we simply look at the facts of the case, the answer will present itself. Both Greek and Hebrew, like French and German today, have in actual fact a second person singular form of the pronoun and of the verb which is in fact normally used to single people. So had Elizabethan English. In Greek and in Hebrew there is nothing at all reverential about the second personal singular, *thee* and *thou*, for they are the normal forms used to address individuals. Again, it is the plain fact that the Bible itself uses the same form to address God and man; in this case the form is *thou*. To David, as the Authorized Version has it, Nathan said: 'Thou art the man' (II Sam. 12.7). The Commandments, addressed to men, begin: 'Thou shalt not.' As a sheer matter of fact, the Bible feels no irreverence and no unnaturalness in addressing God and man by the same pronoun. It is in fact *our* ecclesiastical custom which is unbiblical.

It is only fit and right that a man should speak to God in the language of his own day and generation. What he must bring to God is not the best that people were able to produce centuries ago, but the best that he himself is able to produce in his own time.

It may be that those of us who are older and who have lived within the Church for a life-time have to admit a certain element of selfishness here. We love the old phrases; they are printed on our memories and written on our hearts. They have become so much part of us that we cannot think of worship without them. But the cold fact is that we who are like that are a dwindling race. There has arisen a new generation, and to make worship real for them, worship must be in the language of the twentieth century to meet the need of the twentieth-century man.

That is not to say that the treasures of devotion have to be abandoned and discarded. To do that would be foolish and reckless and ungrateful; and that is why in this book, while we have adopted the language and the idiom of the present, we have always included in each Epilogue one of the great prayers of the past, in the noble liturgical language which is conventional for prayer. The fact that this generation must speak in its own voice is no reason for refusing to listen to the great voices of the past.

2. But we said that there were two levels on which this question of intelligibility arises. There is the simple matter of the pronunciation of words. Marcus Dods, the great Scottish scholar and preacher, once remarked that, when people said that a sermon was a good sermon, in a very high proportion of cases it simply meant that they had heard it. I knew a small boy who had his own version of the Lord's Prayer. He had two petitions all his own: 'Herald be thy name,' and 'Deliver us from eagles!' The picture in the second is indeed vivid, and the first is no doubt somewhere interconnected with the 'herald angels'. A day-school teacher once told me of an incident from her own class, the youngest class in school. They were asked to tell their favourite hymns and then the class sung each one as it was told. George in the back seat was bobbing up and down excitedly awaiting his turn to choose. 'Well, George,' said the teacher, 'what hymn do you want?' 'Four in a bed,' George immediately replied. 'Four in a bed?' the teacher queried in bewilderment. 'Yes, miss,' said George. 'Away in a manger, no crib four in a bed.' George's picture was of a crowded manger with all the holy family in it, and in truth, if

17

we are not careful with our punctuation we do find 'Mary and Joseph and the babe lying in a manger' (Luke 2.16).

These mistakes, and there are many more like them, come quite simply from the faulty enunciation of the leader and the teacher. To be intelligible requires clear language and clear speaking, two things which no leader should ever forget.

(c) In public worship the leader must always try to make his prayers *relevant*. This is simply another way of saying that he must remember that it is not his own prayers but the prayers of the whole group which it is his task and his privilege to bring to God.

It is extraordinary how common this failure in relevance can be. In Scotland they tell a story of a minister who was appointed to a chair in a theological college late in life, and after a long parish ministry. It was his custom frequently to use in his lectures material that he had already used in his sermons. And one day he electrified a class of virile male students by beginning a sentence: 'As those of you who are mothers will be aware.' Few will reach such depths of irrelevance, but much irrelevance there can be.

But there are irrelevancies which are different from such glaring and blatant examples. Perhaps the worst kind of irrelevancy is the irrelevancy which assumes a spiritual experience which the group certainly has never had. This is the kind of irrelevancy which haunts the prayers of those who found everything on the Psalms. The consciousness of sin of the psalmists, the depths which they plumbed, the contrition which flooded their souls, the heights they scaled and the experience of God which they had are not within the sphere of experience of any normal youth group. To pray in that kind of language is simply to pray in terms which are a foreign language to the group.

This is where the leader must think himself into the life and the experience of his group. He must think himself into the problems and the temptations, the work and the leisure, the joys and the sorrows, the triumphs and the disappointments, the loves and the friendships, the games and the pleasures of his group. To take a simple example, there is something very wrong with the pastoral care and the sympathy of the leader, if he does not remember those who are sitting examinations, when the time of examinations comes round, and if he does not remember both those who have defeated the examiners and those whom the examiners have defeated, when the time of results comes. There is something wrong, if he does not remember the boy or the girl who is about to leave home for a new job in a strange town. There is something wrong, if he does not remember the important match in which the team was victorious or defeated. This is far from saying that his prayers must not have a far wider reach and range than that, and that he will not remember the Church, the nation, society, the community, the world, the work of the Church overseas, and those who have gone out to distant places with the message of the Gospel, but it is to say that the real, personal needs of the group are never to be forgotten.

It is in fact a good idea to get the group to write their own prayers. It is a good thing to ask them to say—or, if they do not want to say, to hand it in anonymously on a slip of paper——what they want to thank God for, what they want to say to God that they are sorry for, what they think they need most of all, whom they want God to bless most of all. Out of such lists the group's own liturgy can be constructed—and it will be theirs.

Prayer in a group is not one man praying and the group listening; it is one man speaking to God the prayers of the group. And that situation cannot happen unless the prayers are relevant to the needs of the group, however far they may also reach out beyond the group.

(d) The leader of a group must make his prayers *concrete* and *detailed*. Here we come upon something which might almost be called a controversy in method. There are those who, as I do, believe that prayer should be detailed and personal and concrete. There are those—and there is a very great deal to be said for this point of view—who hold that prayer should be in the most general terms, and that into the general terms the worshipper should insert his own particular situation. We may take as two magnificent examples of this point of view the General Thanksgiving and the General Confession from the Book of Common Order.

Almighty God, Father of all mercies, we thine unworthy servants do give thee most humble and hearty thanks for all thy goodness and loving-kindness to us, and to all men. We bless thee for our creation, preservation and all the blessings

19

of this life; but above all, for thine inestimable love in the redemption of the world by our Lord Jesus Christ; for the means of grace and the hope of glory. And, we beseech thee, give us that due sense of all thy mercies, that our hearts may be unfeignedly thankful, and that we show forth thy praise, not only with our lips, but in our lives; by giving up ourselves to thy service, and by walking before thee in holiness and righteousness all our days.

Almighty and most merciful Father; we have erred and strayed from thy ways like lost sheep. We have followed too much the devices and desires of our own hearts. We have offended against thy holy laws. We have left undone the things we ought to have done; and we have done those things which we ought not to have done. But thou, O Lord, have mercy upon us. Spare thou them, O God, which confess their faults. Restore thou them that are penitent; according to thy promises declared unto mankind in Christ Jesus our Lord. And grant, O most merciful Father, for his sake, that we may hereafter live a godly, righteous, and sober life to the glory of thy holy name.

In these prayers there is no detail whatsoever. Individual and particular sins are not confessed, and individual and particular gifts are not specified. The idea is that into these general terms the worshipper should insert his own thanksgivings and his own confessions and his own self-dedication.

There is no doubt that for the mature Christian, instructed in prayer, and knowing the intention of these prayers, these prayers are the greatest of all prayers. But it takes years of education in devotion to bring a group to this level, and since there are always new people coming into it, the group will never all be at this level. We are not for a moment saying that such prayers should not be used, and that the use of them should not be taught and explained to the group; but we do say that for the ordinary youth group the prayer which is concrete and detailed will be much more real.

Since it is impossible that the needs of all can be mentioned on any one occasion, it is important that the leader should see to it that over a period all needs are mentioned, in addition to the particular needs which he knows to exist in particular cases at the moment.

It is told that on one occasion a little girl after hearing Spurgeon preach said to her mother: 'How does that man know what goes on in our house?' To use the modern slang, the words of the preacher were 'spot on'! A. J. Gossip used to love to tell how once after a service an oldish man came to thank him for a service which had meant much to him. Gossip said to him: 'I wonder if you would mind telling me what it is about the service which has meant so much to you?' The man answered: 'I am old man now and I am a lawyer. And I have been coming to church for far more than half a century and never until today did I hear lawyers as a profession prayed for!' Somewhere in his intercessory prayer Gossip had remembered those whose task it was to make and to administer, to expound and to explain the law, and the old man had felt himself and his profession lifted up to God.

Prayer, especially with young people, should be such that every now and again each one of them will say: 'This means me!' No one would ever wish to banish from worship the great general prayers of the Church, but there is everything to be said for a concrete detail in which every now and then each individual person will feel himself personally remembered before God.

(e) Last of the things to which the leader must see is something very simple, but something often forgotten. The leader must see to it that he is *brief*. In the Lord's Prayer in English there are only seventy words, including the ascription of praise and the Amen. There are few prayers, few addresses, few sermons, few lectures, and few services which would not benefit from being shorter. To run over time is simply bad workmanship and the result of inadequate preparation. If the Epilogue is to last ten minutes, it should last ten minutes and not a minute more. If a man is broadcasting, and if he is allocated fifteen minutes of broadcasting time, he will take that fifteen minutes and no more, for he knows quite well that, if he overruns, he will simply be faded out. No one need say that he cannot be shorter; he would be shorter, if he had to be.

In the first place, it is far better to leave people when they are still wanting more than to go on until they are wishing the leader would stop. And in the second place, the capacity of the

21

human mind for concentrated attention is strictly limited. There is hardly anyone who is able to concentrate for as long as two minutes. If the reader does not believe this, let him try to think of one thing, *and of nothing else*, for two minutes, and, unless he has a quite exceptionally well-trained and disciplined mind, he will find it quite impossible. All kinds of thoughts and pictures will invade his mind, and his concentration will be broken.

It is not only courteous to keep to the time allocated, it is also the way to be effective.

There remains one question which has to be asked, but which cannot be certainly answered. Who is to conduct the Epilogue? Is the leader to conduct the Epilogue every evening? If there is a minister or chaplain available is he to be brought in? Or, are members of the group at least sometimes to conduct it? There are two distinct lines by which the answer to this question must be approached, and there are two answers, each equally valid. On the one hand, it is important that the Epilogue should be conducted as well as it possibly can be. One of the results of religious broadcasting is that it has set a standard, by which all other occasions tend to be judged. From that point of view, it may be well that the leader or the chaplain should conduct the Epilogue. But on the other hand, for a member of the group to conduct the Epilogue is an invaluable act of witness, and there is often more reality in a stumbling and hesitating attempt which is utterly sincere than in the polished, but professional, performance of the expert. This is something which the leader will have to decide for himself in the circumstances of his own group. But one thing is certain, the leader will have done a magnificent job, if in the end almost any member of the group is willing and able to lead the act of worship which closes the group's activities.

We have kept to the end the most important question of all —the place of the Epilogue in the activities of the group. The Epilogue can have very different places in the activities of the group. It can be a mere convention, a sop to religion, something done because it would displease the church authorities who provide the premises, if it was not done. It can be a mere addendum to the night's proceedings. It can be a duty, accepted but by no means welcomed. It can be a formality, duly discharged, but very much on the circumference of the group's activities. Beyond all doubt the Epilogue should be at the very centre of the life of the group; it should be the mainspring of the activities of the group; it should be that which creates the atmosphere in which all the other activities of the group take place. Now, if this is so the attitude of the leader himself is of supreme importance. If it is not real to him, it will not be real to the group. The last thing he should do is to be in any sense or in any way apologetic about the Epilogue. In a certain kind of group it is very easy for the leader to approach the Epilogue apologetically. His attitude will say: 'If you don't mind, and if you will be patient for a moment or two, we will have the Epilogue now. I know it's a bit of a nuisance, and I know that you are not very interested, but it's "the done thing" so let's have it and get it over.' That attitude will inevitably communicate itself to the group. There must be no apologies, and the leader must make it quite clear that he is not asking the Epilogue time as a favour, but that he is claiming it as a right, and that he himself believes that it is in this act of worship that the activities of the group culminate, and that it is on it that the fellowship of the group depends.

And let the leader remember that an act of worship can never be out of place. Many of the most memorable acts of worship that I myself have seen and participated in have come at the end, for instance, of a dance or a party when all gathered round to pray before they went out to their own roads. There is no healthy and clean pleasure and activity in which prayer and worship are out of place. Jesus himself was just as much at home at a wedding feast as he was in the temple or in the synagogue. If the leader is quite certain that this is the peak of the evening, and if he approaches it as a perfectly natural activity, no matter what has gone before, then the Epilogue has at least been given its rightful place in the activities of the group —and that is more than half way to ensuring that it has its true effect. And then it may be that in these few moments of worship young people will really and truly find Jesus Christ, and that is what the Epilogue ultimately is for.

# ALL OF LIFE

*A Prayer of William Bright for the right spirit in worship*

Almighty God, from whom every good prayer cometh, and who pourest out on all who desire it the spirit of grace and supplication: deliver us, when we draw nigh to thee, from coldness of heart and wanderings of mind, that with steadfast thoughts and kindled affections we may worship thee in spirit and in truth: through Jesus Christ our Lord.  Amen.

*The Reading Lesson:* Luke 18.9-14

*Prayer*

O God, our Father, our life reaches out in ever-widening circles; bless us in each one of them.

Bless us in our homes and help us to remember all that we owe to them.

Bless us in our school and help us to learn well and to play fair.

Bless us in our university and college and help us to use to the full every opportunity which is given to us to equip our minds with knowledge and to widen our horizons.

Bless us in the place where we work and help us to be workmen who will never need to be ashamed of anything they do or make.

Bless us in our town and help us to put as much and more into the life of the community as we take out.

Bless us in our church; make us in our church to worship with reverence and with gladness to serve the church with whatever gifts we have.

Bless us in our country, and help us to study, to learn and to train that we may be good citizens of it.

Bless us in the world, and in our day bind the nations together in peace.

## A Prayer from the Coptic Liturgy of St Cyril

O God of love, who hast given us a new commandment through thine only-begotten Son, that we should love one another, even as thou didst love us the unworthy and the wandering, and gavest thy beloved Son for our life and salvation: we pray thee give us, thy servants, in all time of our life on earth, a mind forgetful of past ill-will, a pure conscience, sincere thoughts and a heart to love our brethren: for the sake of Jesus Christ, thy Son, our Lord and Saviour. Amen.

## The Blessing

The grace of the Lord Jesus Christ be with us all.  Amen.

*The Opening Prayer*

O God, our Father, give us tonight and at all times,

> Minds which are eager to seek;
> Memories which are strong to remember;
> Wills which are dedicated to obey;
> Hearts which are surrendered to love;
> Lives which are committed to service:

through Jesus Christ our Lord.   Amen.

*The Reading Lesson:* Luke 6.12-16

*Prayer*

Let us think of the names by which Jesus called his people.

He called them disciples, which means learners.

> Lord Jesus, help us day by day to learn more of this world's knowledge and more of your love, so that day by day we may become better equipped to be the servants of our fellow men, and so that day by day we may be more firmly bound to you.

He called them witnesses.

> Lord Jesus, help us never to be ashamed to show to all men that we belong to you, and grant that our lives may shine like lights in this dark world to lead others to you.

He called them apostles, which means ambassadors.

> Lord Jesus, help us to remember that you are sending us out to live and to speak for you and help us so to live that we shall always bring credit on the name we bear, and so that others may find in us the way to you.

He called them his friends.

> Lord Jesus, you loved us so much that you died for us. Help us to be loyal and true to you as friends should be and never at any time to let you down.

## A Prayer of Queen Anne

Almighty and Eternal God, the Disposer of all the affairs in the world, there is not one circumstance so great as not to be subject to thy power, nor so small but it comes within thy care; thy goodness and wisdom show themselves through all thy works, and thy loving kindness and mercy appear in the several dispensations of thy Providence. May we readily submit ourselves to thy pleasure and sincerely resign our wills to thine, with all patience, meekness and humility: through Jesus Christ our Lord. Amen.

## The Blessing

May God the Father bless us. May Christ the Son take care of us. The Holy Spirit enlighten us all the days of our life.

The Lord be our defender and keeper of body and soul now and for ever and to the ages of ages. Amen.

# RESPECT AND REVERENCE

*The Opening Prayer*

Help us, O God, to find here tonight,
 Wisdom to know what is right,
 And strength to do what is right.
Enlighten our minds with your truth;
Warm our hearts with your love;
Fill our lives with your power,
 That we may go out to live for you: through Jesus
 Christ our Lord.  Amen.


*The Reading Lesson:* 1 Corinthians 12.12-27


*Prayer*

Give us, O God, at all times respect for ourselves,
 So that we may never do work of which we would be
 ashamed;
 So that we may never stoop to that which is mean and
 low;
 So that we may never do in the present that which in
 the future we would have cause to regret.

Give us, O God, at all times love for others,
 So that we may never refuse an appeal for help;
 So that we may help even before we are asked for help;
 So that we may never do anything which would injure or
 hurt anyone else in body or in mind;
 So that we may find our joy in service and not in selfish-
 ness; in giving and not in getting; in sharing and not in
 keeping.

Give us, O God, at all times reverence for you,
So that we may remember that wherever we are and whatever we do you see us;
So that we may always obey your commands;
So that we may fear nothing except to grieve you, and seek nothing except to please you.

## A Prayer of Ludwig von Beethoven

We must praise thy goodness, that thou hast left nothing undone to draw us to thyself. But one thing we ask of thee, our God, not to cease thy work in our improvement. Let us tend towards thee, no matter by what means, and be fruitful in good works, for the sake of Jesus Christ our Lord. Amen.

## The Blessing

May grace, mercy and peace, from God the Father, Son, and Holy Spirit, be with us all now and evermore. Amen.

# FOR THOSE IN TROUBLE

*A Prayer from John Calvin before listening to God's Word*

O Lord, Heavenly Father, in whom is the fulness of light and of wisdom, enlighten our minds by the Holy Spirit, and give us grace to receive thy Word with reverence and humility, without which no man can understand thy truth. For Christ's sake, Amen.

*The Reading Lesson:* Psalm 95.1-7

*Prayer*

O God, our Father, bless those for whom life is very difficult.

Those who have difficult decisions to make, and who honestly do not know what is the right thing to do;

Those who have difficult tasks to do and to face, and who fear that they may fail in them;

Those who have difficult temptations to face, and who know only too well that they may fall to them, if they try to meet them alone;

Those who have a difficult temperament and nature to master, and who know that they can be their own worst enemies;

Those who have difficult people to work with, those who have to suffer unjust treatment, unfair criticism, unappreciated work.

Those who are sad because some one they loved has died;

Those who are disappointed in something for which they hoped very much;

Those who have been hurt by the malice of their enemies, or, what is far more bitter, by the faithlessness and the disloyalty of their friends.

30

Bless us all tonight, O God, with whatever need we come to you.

*A Prayer of Dean Henry Alford*

O Lord, give us more charity, more self-denial, more likeness to thee. Teach us to sacrifice our comforts to others, and our likings for the sake of doing good. Make us kindly in thought, gentle in word, generous in deed. Teach us that it is better to give than to receive; better to forget ourselves than to put ourselves forward; better to minister than to be ministered unto. And unto thee, the God of Love, be all the glory and praise, both now and for evermore.　Amen.

*The Blessing*

The grace of the Lord Jesus Christ, the love of God, and the fellowship of the Holy Spirit be with us all.　Amen.

# OURSELVES AND OTHERS

*The Opening Prayer*

O God, our Father, we have come to you tonight that you may make us able,

> To walk in your light;
> To act in your strength;
> To think in your wisdom;
> To speak in your truth;
> To live in your love;

so that when all the days are done we may come to dwell in your glory: through Jesus Christ our Lord. Amen.

*The Reading Lesson:* Matthew 7.1-12

*Prayer*

O God, our Father, you have told us that we must not judge others, if we ourselves do not want to be judged. Help us never to be too critical of each other.

Keep us from harshly criticizing the work of others, and help us to remember that we have no right to criticize anyone's work, unless we are prepared to do the job better, or at least give a hand with it.

Keep us from unsympathetically criticizing the pleasures of others. Help us to remember that different people have different ways of enjoying themselves, that different people like different kinds of music and games and books, and different ways of spending their leisure. Help us not to despise everything which we don't like.

Keep us from contemptuously or arrogantly criticizing the beliefs of others. Help us to remember that there are as many ways to the stars as there are men to climb them;

and help us never to laugh at anyone's belief, if that is the way he gets to God.

Help us always,

> To praise rather than to criticize;
> To sympathize rather than to condemn;
> To encourage rather than to discourage;
> To build up rather than to destroy;
> To think of people at their best rather than
>    at their worst.

## A Prayer from the Fifth Century Liturgy of Malabar

Grant, O God, that the ears which have heard the voice of thy songs may be closed to the voice of clamour and dispute; that the eyes which have seen thy great love may also behold thy blessed hope; that the tongues which have sung thy praise may speak the truth; that the feet which have walked thy courts may walk in the region of light; that the bodies which have partaken of thy living Body may be restored to newness of life. Glory be to thee for thine unspeakable gift. Amen.

## The Blessing

The grace of the Lord Jesus Christ be with us all. Amen.

# THE GIFT AND THE TASK

*The Opening Prayer*

O God, you have said that you are specially near to those who are childlike in heart. Give us tonight,

A child's trust, that we may never doubt your love;

A child's wonder, that we may be lost in wonder at the beauty and the bounty of the universe and at the miracle of your love for us;

A child's love, that we may love you as a child ought to love a father:

through Jesus Christ our Lord. Amen.

*The Reading Lesson:* Matthew 18.1-6

*Prayer*

Help us, O God, at all times to do the things we ought to do. To that end give us,

Clear sight,

that we may know what to do;

Courage,

to embark upon it;

Skill,

to find a way through all its problems;

Perseverance,

to bring it to its appointed end;

Strength,

to resist all the temptations which would seek to lure us aside.

So help us to begin, to continue and to end all things in you.

*A Prayer of Dean Colet*

O most merciful Father, who dost put away the sins of those who truly repent, we come before thy throne in the name of Jesus Christ, that for his sake alone, thou wilt have compassion upon us, and let not our sins be a cloud between thee and us. Amen.

*The Blessing*

The peace of God which passeth all understanding keep our hearts and minds in the knowledge and love of God, and of his Son Jesus Christ our Lord, and the blessing of God Almighty, the Father, the Son and the Holy Spirit, be amongst us and remain with us always. Amen.

# FOR THOSE WE REMEMBER

*The Opening Prayer*

Teach us this night, O God,
 how to master ourselves,
  that we may serve others.
And help us this night so to see you, that through all the
days of the week we may never forget you: through Jesus
Christ our Lord. Amen.

*The Reading Lesson:* Isaiah 1.12-18

*Prayer*

O God, our Father,

 Bless our friends and our loved ones and keep them safe
  from harm and danger.
 Bless our enemies and those who dislike us, and help us
  by caring for them to make them our friends.
 Bless those who are in pain of body, anxiety of mind,
  and sorrow of heart.
 Bless those who are lonely because death has taken a dear
  one from them.
 Bless those who are old and who now are left alone.
 Bless those who have made a mess of life and who know
  well that they have no one but themselves to blame.
 Bless those who have fallen to temptation and who are
  sorry now, and give them grace to begin again and this
  time not to fall.
 Bless all who are in trouble and help them to win their
  way through it.

Bless each one of us as you know we need.

## A Prayer of John Tillotson

Give us, O Lord, a mind after thine own heart, that we may delight to do thy will, O our God; and let thy law be written on our hearts. Give us courage and resolution to do our duty, and a heart to be spent in thy service, and in doing all the good that possibly we can the few remaining days of our pilgrimage here on earth. Grant this, we humbly beseech thee, for the sake of Jesus Christ thy Son our Lord. Amen.

## The Blessing

And now may the blessing of the Lord rest and remain upon all his people in every land and of every tongue. The Lord meet in mercy all that seek him. The Lord comfort all that suffer and mourn. The Lord hasten his coming, and now give us and all his people peace. Amen.

# A THANKSGIVING FOR PEOPLE

*The Opening Prayer*

O God, our Father, we come to you tonight to find,
> Strength,
>> To keep our hearts pure;
>> To keep our minds clean;
>> To keep our words true;
>> To keep our deeds kind:

through Jesus Christ our Lord.   Amen.

*The Reading Lesson:* Psalm 119.9-16

*Prayer*

Tonight, O God, we bring our thanks to you, and specially our thanks for people.

For those who are an example to us, and those who in their lives show us what life ought to be;

For those who are an inspiration to us, and who fill us with the desire to make of life a noble thing;

For those who are a comfort to us when life has hurt us;

For those who are a strength to us, and in whose company we feel fit to tackle any task;

For those who, although we do not know them personally, have by their words or by their writings influenced us for good;

For those whose love and care and service and understanding we so often take for granted;

For those who give us loyal friendship and for those who give us true love:
> We this night thank you, O God.

And most of all we thank you for Jesus to be the Pattern of our lives, the Companion of our way, and the Saviour of our souls.

*A Prayer of Richard Baxter*

O thou Spirit of Life, breathe upon thy graces in us, take us by the hand and lift us up from earth, that we may see what glory thou hast prepared for them that love thee: through Jesus Christ our Lord. Amen.

*The Blessing*

Unto God's gracious mercy and protection we commit ourselves. The Lord bless and keep us. The Lord make his face to shine upon us and be gracious unto us. The Lord lift up the light of his countenance upon us, and give us peace, both now and evermore. Amen.

# FOR ALL WRONG THINGS

*The Opening Prayer*

*A Prayer of B. F. Westcott before reading the Bible*

Blessed Lord, by whose providence all holy Scriptures were written and preserved for our instruction, give us grace to study them this and every day, with patience and love. Strengthen our souls with the fulness of their divine teaching. Keep from us all pride and irreverence. Guide us in the deep things of thy heavenly wisdom, and of thy great mercy lead us by thy word unto everlasting life: through Jesus Christ our Lord and Saviour. Amen.

*The Reading Lesson:* Luke 4.16-22

*Prayer*

O God, our Father, we have come to you tonight to say that we are sorry for all the wrong things that we have done.

    For the work that we did carelessly;
    For the work that we have left half-finished;
    For the work that we have not even begun:
        Forgive us, O God.

    For the people we have hurt;
    For the people we have disappointed;
    For the people we have failed when they needed us most:
        Forgive us, O God.

    For the friends to whom we have been disloyal;
    For the loved ones to whom we have been untrue;
    For the promises we have broken;
    For the vows we have forgotten:
        Forgive us, O God.

For the way in which we have disobeyed you;
For the way in which we have grieved you;
For our failure to love you as you have loved us:
>    Forgive us, O God.

## A Prayer of Polycarp

May God the Father, and the eternal High Priest, Jesus
Christ, build us up in faith and truth and love, and grant to
us our portion among the saints with all those who believe
on our Lord Jesus Christ. We pray for all saints, for kings
and rulers, for the enemies of the Cross of Christ, and for
ourselves we pray that our fruit may abound and we may be
made perfect in Christ Jesus our Lord.   Amen.

## The Blessing

May grace, mercy, and peace, from Father, Son, and Holy
Spirit, one God, rest upon us all now and abide with each
one of us henceforth and for evermore.   Amen.

# THOSE TO WHOM WE MATTER

*The Opening Prayer*

Lord Jesus, we know that you have rest for the tired.

Lord Jesus, we know that you have guidance for the perplexed.

Lord Jesus, we know that you have strength for the tempted.

Give us tonight your rest, your guidance, and your strength.
This we ask for your love's sake. Amen.

*The Reading Lesson:* Matthew 11.25-30

*Prayer*

O God, our Father, help us to remember that you know all about us.

Keep our thoughts so clean and pure that they may be fit for you to see.

Help us so to live that even our secret actions, the things we do when there is no man to see, may be fit to be open to your sight.

O God, our Father, we know that there are those who love us.

Help us never to do anything to hurt or disappoint them.

Help us never to do anything which would make us less fit to be loved.

O God, our Father, we know that there are those on whom we have an influence.

Help us never to do anything which would make it easier for them to go wrong.

Help us never to place temptation in their way.

Help us to remember that there are things in this world which cost too much, and that there are pleasures which can be too dearly bought. And help us to live so that life may be ever stronger and purer and kinder day by day, so that at the end of the days there may be nothing of which to be ashamed and nothing to regret.

## A Prayer of Mohammed

O Lord, grant us to love thee; grant that we may love those that love thee; grant that we may do the deeds that win thy love. Make the love of thee to be dearer to us than ourselves, our families, than wealth, and even than cool water. Amen.

## The Blessing

The love of God, the grace of our Lord Jesus Christ, the fellowship of the Holy Spirit be with us all, now and always. Amen.

# RIGHT RELATIONSHIPS

*The Opening Prayer*

We have come to you tonight, O God,
>    To thank you for your past gifts to us;
>    To receive strength for the present duties we must do;
>    To find courage to face anything which the future may
>       bring.

So let it be given unto us: through Jesus Christ our Lord.
   Amen.

*The Reading Lesson:* Proverbs 8.12-21

*Prayer*

O God, our Father, help us in our lives to have the right
attitude to everyone.

Help us to have the right attitude to ourselves.
Keep us from
>    The pride which makes us conceitedly pleased with
>       ourselves;
>    The false modesty which is an excuse for evading re-
>       sponsibility;
>    The blindness which cannot see our own faults;
>    The selfishness which puts self in the centre of every-
>       thing.

Help us to have the right attitude to others.
Keep us from
>    The critical spirit which looks for faults;
>    The thoughtless spirit which never thinks of the feel-
>       ings of others;
>    The cowardice which is afraid of what others will say;

The desire to curry favour which makes us too intent
on pleasing others, even at the expense of honour, of
honesty and of truth.

Help us to have the right attitude to you.
Keep us from
The forgetfulness which never thinks of you;
The rebelliousness which takes its own way of things;
The irreverence which forgets that you are here.
Help us to think of ourselves, to think of others, and to
think of you as we ought.

*A Prayer of J. H. Jowett*

O God, our Father, we would thank thee for all the bright
things of life. Help us to see them, and to count them, and
to remember them, that our lives may flow in ceaseless
praise: for the sake of Jesus Christ our Lord. Amen.

*The Blessing*

The love of God, the grace of the Lord Jesus Christ, the
fellowship of the Holy Spirit be with us all, now and evermore. Amen.

# TO GET RID OF AND TO GET

*The Opening Prayer*

O God, our Father, silence everything in us this night which would keep us from hearing what you have to say to us. Control our minds, that all our thoughts may be concentrated on you. And help us to find here light to shine upon our path and strength to walk in it: through Jesus Christ our Lord. Amen.

*The Reading Lesson:* Matthew 25.1-13

*Prayer*

O God, our Father, save us from everything which would make life useless and ugly.

Save us from,

> The unteachable spirit which will not learn;
> The ungrateful spirit which never says thanks;
> The unhappy spirit which is filled with complaints and discontent.

Save us from,

> The disobliging spirit which grudges any help it has to give;
> The discourteous spirit which never thinks of the feelings of anyone else;
> The disobedient spirit which will take nothing but its own way.

Give us,

> A sense of responsibility,
> > that we may know that we can neither live nor die to ourselves:

A sense of duty,
> that we may leave nothing that we ought to do undone;

A sense of gratitude,
> that we may offer thanks to you by trying to live more nearly as you would have us to do.

## A Prayer of Peter Marshall

O God, our Father, let us not be content to wait and see what will happen, but give us the determination to make the right things happen.

While time is running out, save us from the patience which is akin to cowardice.

Give us the courage to be either hot or cold, to stand for something, lest we fall for anything. In Jesus' Name. Amen.

## The Blessing

The blessing of God, Father, Son and Holy Spirit, be upon us all now and stay with each one of us always. Amen.

# THE PRICE OF THE PRECIOUS

*The Opening Prayer*

Give us this night, O Father,
    Reverence,
        to realize your presence;
    Humility,
        to know our own need;
    Trust,
        to ask your help;
    Obedience,
        to accept whatever you say to us:
so that it may this night be good for us to be here: through
Jesus Christ our Lord.   Amen.

*The Reading Lesson:* Matthew 16.24-27

*Prayer*

Help us, O God, to remember that all great things have their
price.

Help us to remember that,
    There is no achievement without work;
    There is no learning without study;
    There is no skill of body or of mind without discipline.

Help us to remember that,
    There is no purity without vigilance;
    There is no friendship without loyalty;
    There is no love without the death of self.

Help us to remember that,
    There is no joy without service;
    There is no discipleship without devotion;
    There is no crown without a cross.

So help us to be willing to pay the price that we may enter into our reward.

## An Intercession from the Liturgy of St Mark

We most earnestly beseech thee, O thou lover of mankind, to bless all thy people, the flocks of thy fold. Send down into our hearts the peace of heaven, and grant us also the peace of this life. Give life to the souls of all of us, and let no deadly sin prevail against us, or any of thy people. Deliver all who are in trouble, for thou art our God, who settest the captives free; who givest hope to the hopeless and help to the helpless; who liftest up the fallen; and who art the haven of the shipwrecked. Give thy pity, pardon and refreshment to every Christian soul, whether in affliction or error. Preserve us in our pilgrimage through this life from hurt and danger, and grant that we may end our lives as Christians, well-pleasing to thee and free from sin, and that we may have our portion and lot with all thy saints: for the sake of Jesus Christ, our Lord and Saviour. Amen.

## The Blessing

The grace of the Lord Jesus Christ be with us all. Amen.

*The Opening Prayer*

O God, our Father, tonight we come to you to listen and to learn.
Take from us
> The laziness which will not learn,
> The prejudice which cannot learn,

and give us
> Minds adventurous to think,
> Memories strong to remember,
> Wills resolute to do.

This we ask for Jesus' sake.  Amen.

*A Collect from the Book of Common Prayer for use before reading Scripture*

Blessed Lord, who hast caused all holy Scriptures to be written for our learning; Grant that we may in such wise hear them, read, mark and inwardly digest them, that by patience, and comfort of thy holy Word, we may embrace and ever hold fast the blessed hope of everlasting life which thou hast given us in our Saviour Jesus Christ.  Amen.

*The Reading Lesson:* Romans 8.31-39

*Prayer*

O God, Lord of all good life, give us the things which will enable us to make something worthwhile out of life.

Discipline to accept the necessity of study and of work;
A sense of proportion to see the things which really matter;

The ability to take the long view that we may never sell the most precious things for a moment's cheap pleasure:
Grant us these things, O God.

Perseverance that we may never leave a task uncompleted;
Concentration that we too may say, This one thing I do;
Patience that we may never give up and never give in:
Grant us these things, O God.

The teachable spirit which realizes its own ignorance;
The humble spirit which will accept advice and which will not resent rebuke;
The diligent spirit that whatever our hand finds to do we may do with our might:
Grant us these things, O God.

So help us to bear the yoke in our youth that in the days to come we may serve you and serve our fellowmen well: through Jesus Christ our Lord.

*The Blessing*

The blessing of God, Father, Son and Holy Spirit be on us now and stay with us always. Amen.

*The Opening Prayer*

Give us this night, O God,

      Ears open to hear your word;

      Minds ready to accept your truth;

      Wills ready to accept your commands;

      And above all hearts ready to answer to your love:

through Jesus Christ our Lord.   Amen.

*The Reading Lesson:* Luke 4.14-30

*Prayer*

So faith, hope, love abide, these three; but the greatest of these is love.

O God, our Father, grant us

  The faith which is sure and certain of what it believes;

  The faith which unhesitatingly believes in your promises
    and unquestioningly accepts your commands;

  The faith which is loyal to you in any situation.

  The hope which will never despair;

  The hope that no disappointment can quench;

  The hope which in spite of failure will never give in.

  The love which is always ready to forgive;

  The love which is always eager to help;

  The love which is always happier to give than to get.

And so grant that living in faith, in hope, in love, we may live like Jesus.

*A Prayer of Thomas Arnold*

O Lord, we have a busy world around us. Eye, ear, and thought will be needed for all our work to be done in the world. Now ere we again enter into it, we would commit eye, ear, and thought to thee. Do thou bless them and keep their work thine, that as through thy natural laws our hearts beat and our blood flows without any thought of ours for them, so our spiritual life may hold on its course at those times when our minds cannot consciously turn to commit each particular thought to thy service: through Jesus Christ our Lord. Amen.

*The Blessing*
The grace of the Lord Jesus Christ be with us all. Amen.

*The Opening Prayer*

O God, our Father, help us tonight,
>    To see ourselves in all our weakness,
>    To see you in all your power.

Then help us to take our weakness to your power, that in your love you may give us strength to do the things we cannot do, and to be the things we cannot be: through Jesus Christ our Lord.   Amen.

*The Reading Lesson:* Galatians 6.1-10

*Prayer*

Tonight, O God, we want to forget ourselves and to remember others.

>    Those who are ill and in pain;
>    Those who are waiting for an operation;
>    Those who are waiting for a doctor's diagnosis and verdict and who fear the worst:
>>        Bless all such.

>    Those who are nervous, worried, anxious, afraid of life;
>    Those who are on the verge of a nervous breakdown;
>    Those who feel that they cannot cope with life:
>>        Bless all such.

>    Those who are hungry and cold;
>    Those who are refugees with no home;
>    Those who are unemployed with no work;
>    Those who are persecuted and those who have lost their freedom:
>>        Bless all such.

Out of your great riches supply the need of those distressed in body, mind or heart.

## A Prayer of Thomas à Kempis

Grant that in all things we may behave ourselves so as befits a creature to his Creator, a servant to his Lord. Make us diligent in all our duties, watchful against all temptations, pure and temperate and moderate in thy most lawful enjoyments, that they may never become a snare to us. Help us, O Lord, to act towards our neighbour that we may never transgress the royal law of thine, of loving him as ourselves. Finally, we beseech thee, O Lord, to sanctify us throughout, that our whole spirit, soul and body, may be preserved blameless unto the coming of the Lord Jesus Christ: to whom with thee and the Holy Spirit be all honour and glory for ever. Amen.

## The Blessing

The grace of the Lord Jesus Christ, the love of God, the fellowship of the Holy Spirit be with us all this night and stay with us always. Amen.

# THE NECESSARY KNOWLEDGE

*The Opening Prayer*

O God, our Father, the life of all who live, the strength of the weak, and the hope of all who are in distress, put this night your truth into our minds and your purity into our hearts. Strengthen our wills that we may be able always to choose the right and always to refuse the wrong. And help us at all times to bear one another's burdens and to forgive one another's faults that we may obey your law and become daily more like our blessed Lord. This we ask for your love's sake. Amen.

*The Reading Lesson:* Ecclesiastes 7.1-12

*Prayer*

O God, our Father, give us the knowledge which will enable us to live life well.

Help us really to know ourselves. Help us to know
Our own ignorance, that we may ever be teachable and willing to learn;
Our own weakness, that we may be ever on our guard against the temptations which so easily overcome us, unless we are on the watch;
Our own strength, that we may use to the full the gifts and talents which you have given to us.

Help us really to know our fellowmen. Help us to know
That they are your children, so that we may ever respect and reverence all men as sons of God;
That they are our brothers, so that, as members of one great family, we may ever be ready to help one another;

That there is so much bad in the best of us and so much good in the worst of us that it ill becomes any of us to find fault with the rest of us.

Help us really to know you. Help us to know
Your holiness, that we may know that fear which is the beginning of wisdom;
Your purity, that we also being pure in heart may see you;
Your love, that we may love you as you have first loved us.

*A Prayer of Rabindranath Tagore*

When the heart is hard and parched up, come upon me with a shower of mercy.

When grace is lost from life, come with a burst of song.

When tumultuous work raises its din on all sides, shutting me out from beyond, come to me, my Lord of silence, with thy peace and rest.

When my beggarly heart sits crouched, shut up in a corner, break open the door, my king, and come with the ceremony of a king.

When desire blinds the mind with delusion and dust, O thou holy One, thou wakeful, come with thy light and with thy thunder.

*The Blessing*

The grace of the Lord Jesus Christ be with us all. Amen.

*The Opening Prayer*

Give us tonight, O God,

> Wisdom to know;
> Humility to accept;
> Strength to do

your will for us, so that, having walked in faith, in obedience and in fidelity, we may one day hear you say: Well done! : through Jesus Christ our Lord. Amen.

*The Reading Lesson:* Luke 12.35-48

*Prayer*

Let us pray to God to give us the Seven Virtues which men have always thought the greatest virtues of all.

O God, our Father, give us the virtues which will make life strong and lovely.

Fidelity, that we may be for ever true to friendship, to love and to you;

Hope, that not all earth's setbacks and disappointments may ever drive us to despair;

Love, that we may feel towards our fellowmen as you feel to them;

Prudence, that we may be wise to choose, not that which is at the moment attractive, but that which is to our ultimate good;

Justice, that we may never be swayed by passion or by prejudice, but that in honour and in honesty we may be fair to all men;

Courage, that no cowardly and unworthy fear may ever keep us from doing the right thing and taking the right road;

Self-control, that we may be master of every impulse and of every passion, and so able to serve others because we can rule ourselves.

So let your divine grace make beautiful our human life.

### A Prayer of King Alfred

Lord God Almighty, shaper and ruler of all creatures, we pray thee for thy great mercy to guide us to thy will, to make our minds steadfast, to strengthen us against temptation, to put far from us all unrighteousness. Shield us against our foes, seen and unseen; teach us in order that we may inwardly love thee before all things with a clean mind and a clean body. For thou art our Maker and Redeemer, our help and our comfort, our trust and our hope, now and ever. Amen.

### The Ascription of Praise

To God the Father, who loved us, and made us accepted in the Beloved;

To God the Son, who loved us, and loosed us from our sins by his own blood;

To God the Holy Spirit, who sheddeth the love of God abroad in our hearts;

To the one true God be all love and all glory for time and for eternity. Amen.

# FOR THOSE IN NEED

*The Opening Prayer*

Eternal and everblessed God, you have taught us to call you
Father, and you have surrounded us all our lives by your
fatherly love and care. Help us so to live that we may be
sons and daughters who bring joy and not sorrow to their
Father's heart: through Jesus Christ our Lord. Amen.

*The Reading Lesson:* Luke 7.1-10

*Prayer*

Tonight, O God, we pray to you for all those who are in
pain and distress of body or of mind.

Bless those who are ill; be specially near to those who
will never be well again; and ease the pain of those whose
pain is beyond the skill of men to help.

Bless those who are sad, those on whose dearest circle
the chill wind of death has blown, and comfort those
whom no one else can comfort.

Bless those who have had some great disappointment,
Those who have found a friend untrue;
Those who have found a lover faithless;
Those who have failed in something for which they
toiled;
Those to whom life has refused something on which they
set their hearts.

Bless those who are worried,
Those who are worried about their health;
Those who have an insoluble problem which must be
solved;

Those who have a difficult decision which must be taken;
Those who know that they must meet their testing time;
Those who are tempted and who fear that they may fall.

O God, our Father, we remember all this world's unfortunate ones,
Refugees without a home and without a state;
Those who are persecuted for their faith;
Those who are suffering for their loyalty to some principle which is dearer to them than comfort and than life.

Grant that all in trouble may remember your promise that when they pass through the waters you will be with them, and grant that they may find it true.

*A Prayer of the Venerable Bede*

Open our hearts, O Lord, and enlighten us by the grace of thy Holy Spirit, that we may seek what is well-pleasing to thy will; and so order our doings after thy commandments, that we may be found meet to enter into thine unending joys: through Jesus Christ our Lord. Amen.

*The Blessing*

Now may grace, mercy and peace from Father, Son and Holy Spirit, one God, rest upon us all and abide with each one of us henceforth and for evermore. Amen.

# THE IMPORTANT AND THE UNIMPORTANT

*The Opening Prayer, A Prayer before the reading of Scripture*

O Lord Jesus, who hast told us in thy holy Word that thou lovest us, and gavest thy life for us, keep us in that love, and help us more and more to read, love, and understand thy Word, that we may learn of thee, and of the Holy Spirit and of thy Father in heaven. Amen.

*The Reading Lesson:* Luke 12.22-31

*Prayer*

O God, our Father, forgive us that we so often give our best to the wrong things.

Sometimes we put far more enthusiasm and thought and effort into our pleasures and our games and our amusement than we do into our work.

Sometimes we keep our best behaviour for strangers and our worst behaviour for our own homes; and often we treat our nearest and dearest with a discourtesy and a disregard we would never show to strangers.

Sometimes we get irritated and annoyed and angry about things which in our calmer moments we know do not matter.

Sometimes we lose our temper in an argument about trifles.

Sometimes we allow very little things to cause a quarrel with a friend.

Help us to see what is important and what is unimportant, so that we may never forget the things that matter, and so that we may never allow the things which do not matter to matter too much.

*A Prayer of St Augustine*

O Thou, from whom to be turned is to fall,
    to whom to be turned is to rise,
    and in whom to stand is to abide for ever;
Grant us
    in all our duties thy help;
    in all our perplexities thy guidance;
    in all our dangers thy protection;
    and in all our sorrows thy peace:
        through Jesus Christ our Lord.  Amen.

*The Blessing*

Christ, our Saviour, come thou to dwell within us, that we may go forth with the light of thy hope in our eyes, and thy faith and love in our hearts.  Amen.

# OUR FELLOWSHIP

*The Opening Prayer*

O God, our Father, grant to us, not only to know your truth
with our minds, but also to experience it in our hearts, and
to translate it into our lives. So grant to us to know, to love,
and to live the truth: through Jesus Christ our Lord. Amen

*The Reading Lesson:* Isaiah 40.1-8

*Prayer*

Lord Jesus, Master of all good life, help us in this fellowship always to study

> To make our bodies fitter;
> To make our minds keener and better equipped;
> To make our hearts purer.

Help us here to learn

> To be good sons and daughters in our homes;
> To be good citizens of the community in which we
> live;
> To be good scholars and students of our school or
> our college or our university;
> To be good workmen in whatever trade or craft we
> are engaged;
> To be good members of your Church;
> To be good followers and disciples of Jesus.

Help us here to find week by week

> The joy of learning together;
> The joy of playing together;
> The joy of praying together;
> The joy of worshipping together.

Keep far from us anything that would hurt our fellowship or come between us. Banish from us

>The irritable temper;
>The selfish ambition;
>The arrogant intolerance;
>The false disloyalty.

And help us in this place week by week to come closer to one another and closer to you.

*A Prayer of Jeremy Taylor*

O Eternal God, who hast made all things for man, and man for thy glory; sanctify our bodies and souls, our thoughts and our intentions, our words and actions, that whatsoever we shall think or speak or do may be by us designed to the glorification of thy name, and by the blessing it may be effective and successful in the work of God, according as it can be capable. Let our body be a servant of our mind, and both body and spirit servants of Jesus Christ, that doing all things for thy glory here we may be partakers of thy glory hereafter: through Jesus Christ our Lord. Amen.

*The Blessing*

The grace of the Lord Jesus Christ be with us all. Amen.

# SPEAKING AND LISTENING

*The Opening Prayer*

Eternal God, whom to know is life eternal and whom to serve is fulness of joy, help us to know you with our minds, to love you with our hearts, to serve you with our lives, so that our lives may be garrisoned with your peace and radiant with your glory: through Jesus Christ our Lord. Amen.

*The Reading Lesson:* 1 Samuel 3.1-10

*Prayer*

O God, help us tonight to say to you, just as Samuel did: Speak, Lord, your servant is listening. Speak to us the word we need, and help us to hear it.

Speak to us

> The word of encouragement when we are discouraged and depressed;
> The word of warning when we are likely to go astray;
> The word of comfort when life has hurt us;
> The word of guidance when we do not know what to do and where to go;
> The word of strength to enable us to resist our temptations;
> The word of power to make us able for work and ready for any burden.

Whatever word we need, speak it to us now.

Take from us everything which would keep us from hearing your voice.

Take from us

> The inattentive mind and the wandering thoughts;
> The cold heart and the weak will;

The self-will which disregards the truth;

The prejudice which cannot hear or see the truth, but which sees only what it wants to see;

The desire not to be disturbed, which is afraid of the truth.

Help us in this place to hear your word, and to go out and obey it.

## A Prayer of St Basil

O Lord our God, teach us, we beseech thee, to ask thee aright for the right blessings. Steer thou the vessel of our life towards thyself, thou tranquil haven of all storm-tossed souls. Show us the course wherein we should go. Renew a willing spirit within us. Let thy Spirit curb our wayward senses, and guide and enable us unto that which is our true good, to keep thy laws, and in all our works evermore to rejoice in thy glorious and gladdening presence. For thine is the glory and the praise from all thy saints for ever and ever. Amen.

## The Blessing

The blessing of God, the Father, the Son and the Holy Spirit, be on us now and stay with us always. Amen.

# DIFFICULT TO LIVE WITH

*The Opening Prayer*

Make us tonight, O God,

    sorry for our sins and grateful for your gifts;

Make us

    certain of your power and will to help.

So grant that tonight we may find forgiveness for the past, and strength to do better in the future: through Jesus Christ our Lord. Amen.

*The Reading Lesson:* Romans 15.1-6

*Prayer*

O God, forgive us for the faults which make us difficult to live with.

    If we behave as if we were the only people for whom life is difficult;

    If we behave as if we were far harder worked than anyone else;

    If we behave as if we were the only people who were ever disappointed, or the only people who ever got a raw deal;

    If we are far too self-centred and far too full of self-pity:

        Forgive us, O God.

    If we are too impatient to finish the work we have begun;

    If we are too impatient to listen to some one who wants to talk to us, or to give some one a helping hand;

    If we think that other people are fools, and make no attempt to conceal our contempt for them:

        Forgive us, O God.

If we too often rub people the wrong way;
If we spoil a good case by trying to ram it down some-
one's throat;
If we do things that get on people's nerves, and go on
doing them, even when we are asked not to:
Forgive us, O God.

Help us to take the selfishness and the ugliness out of life
and to do better in the days to come.

*A Prayer of St Augustine*

Blessed are all thy saints, O God and King, who have
travelled over the tempestuous sea of this life, and have
made the harbour of peace and felicity. Watch over us who
are still in our dangerous voyage; and remember such as lie
exposed to the rough storms of trouble and temptations.

Frail is our vessel, and the ocean is wide; but, as in thy
mercy thou hast set our course, so steer the vessel of our
life toward the everlasting shore of peace, and bring us at
length to the quiet haven of our heart's desire, where thou,
O our God, art blessed, and livest and reignest for ever and
ever. Amen.

*The Blessing*

May the Lord lead us when we go, and keep us when we
sleep, and talk with us when we wake; and may the peace
of God which passeth all understanding, keep our hearts
and minds in Christ Jesus our Lord. Amen.

# LIFE'S NEEDS

*The Opening Prayer*

O God, our Father, you are the Truth; give us your truth tonight.

Help us to see the truth about ourselves,
that we may see ourselves as we really are, and not as we think we are.

Help us to see the truth about life,
that we may see what we ought to do, and not only what we want to do.

Help us to see the truth about you,
that we may really know your wisdom and your love,

so that we may trust you wholly and obey you fully: through Jesus Christ our Lord.   Amen

*The Reading Lesson:* Matthew 26.6-13

*Prayer*

O God, our Father, give us your help whatever life is like.

In difficulty keep us from discouragement,
and in failure from despair.

In joy help us never to forget to sympathize with others who are sad, and in sorrow help us to hope for the future as well as to remember the past.

In success keep us from conceit,
and when things go well keep us from thinking that we do not need you.

Help us to remember that there is no situation
in which you cannot help us,

And no time in which we do not need your help.

O God, our Father, bless those for whom the evening is a difficult time;

> Those who are so lonely that they do not know what to do;
>
> Those who are so sad that they do not know how to go on;
>
> Those who are in such pain that they are afraid of the night;
>
> Those who are so worried that sleep is impossible;
>
> Those who are in such need that they do not know how the needs of tomorrow can be met.

Bless everyone in trouble of body or of mind as each one needs.

*An Ancient Prayer*

O God, Author of Eternal Light, do thou shed forth continual day upon those who watch for thee, that our lips may praise thee, our life may bless thee, our meditations may glorify thee: through Jesus Christ our Lord. Amen.

*The Blessing*

The grace of the Lord Jesus Christ go with us all. Amen.

# FOR THE PEACE OF THE WORLD

*The Opening Prayer*

O God, our Father, show us tonight the beauty of holiness,
that we may want it more than anything else in this world.

Show us tonight the ugliness of sin, that with our whole
hearts we may hate that which is wrong,

So that, loving holiness and hating sin, we may walk all our
days in beauty, goodness and truth: through Jesus Christ
our Lord. Amen.

*The Reading Lesson:* Isaiah 65.21-25

*Prayer*

Let us tonight pray for the peace of the world.

O God, Father of all men and King of all nations, you
meant men to live as brothers. Take from all men their
hatreds, their suspicions, their distrusts, and help them to
live in friendship together.

O God, Source of all knowledge and of all strength, you
gave men all the powers which they possess. Grant that men
may no longer even think of using the power with which
they have been entrusted for destruction, but that they may
ever seek to use it all for the blessings of peace.

O God, Creator of all that is within the world, you filled the
world with good things. Yet there are still people who are
starving, who are ravaged by disease, who are homeless,
stateless refugees. Help us

> To pray earnestly;
> To work tirelessly;
> To give generously;
> To plan wisely,

to make this world a place where there shall be no more poverty, no more hunger, no more suffering, no more injustice, and no more fear.

O God, Maker and Searcher of the hearts of men, you gave us wills that we might give them back to you. Help us

> To accept your commandments;
> To obey your voice;
> To trust your love;
> To commit ourselves completely and entirely to you.

### A Prayer of Jeremy Taylor

Relieve and comfort, O Lord, all the persecuted and afflicted; speak peace to troubled consciences; strengthen the weak; confirm the strong; instruct the ignorant; deliver the oppressed from him that spoileth him; and relieve the needy that hath no helper; and bring us all, by the waters of comfort and in the ways of righteousness, to the kingdom of rest and glory: through Jesus Christ our Lord. Amen.

### The Blessing

The blessing of God be upon us all now and stay with each one of us this night and always. Amen.

# THAT WE MAY DO WHAT
# WE OUGHT TO DO

*The Opening Prayer*

Lord Jesus, who said, I am the Way,
    Show us tonight the way we ought to go,
Lord Jesus, who said, I am the Truth,
    Show us this night the truth we ought to know.
Lord Jesus, who said, I am the Life,
    Show us tonight what real life is.
This we ask for your love's sake.  Amen.

*The Reading Lesson:* Luke 1.46-55

*Prayer*

O God, our Father, grant that nothing may stop us doing what we ought to do and being what we ought to be.

Grant that,
    Laziness may not stop us doing the work we ought to do;
    Fear may not keep us from taking the stand we ought to take;
    Selfishness may not stop us giving the service we ought to give.

Grant that,
    Ingratitude may not stop us being as grateful as we ought to be;
    Indifference may not stop us caring as we ought to care;
    Self-will may not stop us obeying you as we ought to obey.

Grant that,
    Lack of perseverance may not stop us finishing the things we have begun;

Lack of discipline may not make us take the easy way;
Lack of foresight may not make us choose the things
  which bring nothing but regret.

Grant that,
  Despair may not make us stop trying;
  Discouragement may not make us give up and give in;
  Pessimism may not take our hope away.

Grant us,
>   Such wisdom of mind;
>   Such strength of will;
>   Such devotion of heart,

that we may not even desire to do anything except the
things that please you: through Jesus Christ our Lord.
Amen.

## A Prayer of Lancelot Andrewes

Take us, we pray thee, O Lord of our life, into thy keeping
this night and ever. O thou Light of lights, keep us from
inward darkness; grant us so to sleep in peace, that we may
arise to work according to thy will: through Jesus Christ
our Lord. Amen.

## The Blessing

The blessing of God be on us now and stay with us always.
Amen.

# FOR EACH ONE'S NEED

*The Opening Prayer*

O God, our Father, make us this evening so aware of your presence that,

The thoughtless may be compelled to think;
The ungrateful may be compelled to give thanks;
Those about to do some wrong thing may be restrained;
That the sad may be comforted; the depressed encouraged; the lonely cheered;
And that those who are happy may be still happier:

through Jesus Christ our Lord.  Amen.

*The Reading Lesson:* Matthew 11.25-30

*Prayer*

O God, our Father, there are no two of us here with the same need. You know our needs. Bless us as each one of us needs. Specially bless those who are in the middle of some specially difficult time:

Those who have some specially difficult task to face or some specially difficult examination to sit;
Those who have some specially difficult problem to solve;
Those who have some specially difficult decision to take;
Those who have some specially difficult temptation to resist;
Those who have some specially baffling doubt through which to think their way.

Speak to those who are
Evading some decision;
Shirking some task;
Putting off some duty;

> Playing with fire;
> Wasting their time;
> Throwing away their opportunities.

Tell them that they dare not bring shame to themselves and disappointment to those who love them.

Speak to those who are successful, that they may be kept from all pride and self-conceit; speak to those who are too self-confident, that they may not be riding for a fall; speak to those who are too sure that they are right and too sure that everyone else is wrong, that they may be kept from intolerance. Help those who are shy. Remember those who are in disgrace and in prison, and keep them from despair.

*A Prayer for Consecration*

Our Father, may Christ's spirit of duty and service ennoble all that we do. Inspire us with the faith, that, in ways beyond our knowing, our work is a blessing to others. From day to day may there be nothing in our work of which we shall be ashamed when the sun is set, nor in the eventide of life when our task is done: through Jesus Christ our Lord. Amen.

*The Blessing*

The blessing of God be on us all now, and stay with each one of us always.   Amen.

# LIFE'S OPPORTUNITIES

*The Opening Prayer*

Grant, O God, that these few minutes with you may send us out again

> More kind to others;
> More honest with ourselves;
> More loyal to you:

through Jesus Christ our Lord.  Amen.

*The Reading Lesson:* Matthew 25.14-30

*Prayer*

O God, our Father, you have made life full of opportunities. Help us to miss none of these opportunities when they come to us.

Help us not to miss the opportunities of learning and help us to work, to study, to train, and to accept discipline that we may

> Deepen our lives;
> Enrich our minds;
> Learn our trade;
> Master our craft;
> Be efficient at our job;
> Be equipped for our profession.

Help us never to miss the opportunities of helping others that we may be ready

> To share with the poor;
> To sympathize with the sad;
> To encourage the depressed;
> To help those who have made mistakes back on
> to the rails again;

To lend a hand to those who are finding things
difficult.

Help us never to miss an opportunity to show where we
stand that we may

Set a Christian example wherever we are;

Always make it easier for others to do and be
good, and never make it easier for them to do
any wrong thing;

Always be good advertisements for our faith and
for our church.

So help us to grasp every opportunity you send, and to use
every gift you have given us that we may make life what
you meant it to be.

### A Prayer for the Lord's Day

O Lord, God of our life, who hast given us the rest of this
sacred day; grant that the benediction of its restfulness may
abide upon us throughout the week. Enable us to carry the
influence of its consecration into all we do; let the praises
of our lips rendered to thee this day become praise in our
lives. May the power of thy love be with us in every duty,
that by pureness, by knowledge, and by tenderness we may
glorify thee; through Jesus Christ our Lord. Amen.

### The Blessing

The grace of the Lord Jesus Christ be with us all. Amen.

# TRUE HUMILITY

*The Opening Prayer*

O God, our Father, for this short time of worship direct and control our thoughts that we may think only of you. Grant us

> Reverence as we remember your glory;
> Penitence as we remember your holiness;
> Gratitude as we remember your love.

So grant that we may rise from our worship

> With knowledge deepened;
> With love kindled;
> With strength to live more nearly as we ought:

through Jesus Christ our Lord. Amen.

*The Reading Lesson:* II Corinthians 5.17-21

*Prayer*

O God, our Father, give to us the humility which

> Realizes its ignorance;
> Admits its mistakes;
> Recognizes its need;
> Welcomes advice;
> Accepts rebuke.

Save us from pride in our knowledge, and make us to think of the great ocean of truth all undiscovered before us.

Save us from pride in our achievement, and make us to remember all that we still have to do.

Save us from pride in our performance, and make us to remember how far short of perfection our best must still fall.

Help us in the days ahead,
>    To study with diligence;
>    To learn with eagerness.
And give us
>    A retentive memory to remember that which we have
>        learned;
>    And a resolute will to put it into action.

## A Prayer of Robert Louis Stevenson

Go with each of us to rest; if any awake, temper to them the dark hours of watching; and when the day returns, return to us, our sun and comforter, and call us up with morning faces and with morning hearts, eager to labour, eager to be happy, if happiness should be our portion, and if the day be marked for sorrow, strong to endure it. Amen.

## The Blessing

The grace of the Lord Jesus Christ be with us all.   Amen.

# THE NECESSITIES OF FRIENDSHIP

*The Opening Prayer*

Grant unto us, in our hearts, O God, as we come to you,
>> Gratitude for all your gifts;
>> Sorrow for all our sins;
>> Trust in your power and will to help.
So grant that we may find here tonight:
>> Forgiveness for the past;
>> Strength for the present;
>> Confidence that the future can bring nothing that in
>> your strength we cannot meet:
through Jesus Christ our Lord.   Amen.

*The Reading Lesson:* I Thessalonians 5.12-24

*Prayer*

Keep us, O God, from all the things which make friendship
impossible.

Keep us from
>> The sarcastic tongue;
>> The critical eye;
>> The ears which love malicious gossip;
>> The mind which thinks the worst;
>> The heart whose only love is self-love.

Give us the things which will enable friendship to flourish.
Give us
>> The ability to bear one another's burdens and to for-
>> give one another's faults;
>> The sympathetic, the unselfish and the understand-
>> ing heart;

The temper and the tongue which are always under
control;

The determination to treat others as we would have
them treat us;

The tolerance which can always see the point of view
of others.

Help us to live ever remembering that in you we live and
move and have our being, and that life is always in your
sight.

*An Ancient Prayer from the Gelasian Sacramentary*

O God, who knowest us to be set in the midst of so many
and great dangers, that by reason of the frailty of our nature
we cannot always stand upright, grant to us such strength
and protection as may support us in all dangers and carry
us through all temptations: through Jesus Christ our Lord.
Amen.

*The Blessing*

The grace of the Lord Jesus Christ, the love of God, and
the fellowship of the Holy Spirit be upon us all now and
stay with each one of us this night and always.   Amen.

# THIS WORLD AND THIS LIFE

*The Opening Prayer*

O God, our Father, be with us at our time of worship tonight.

> When we pray, help us to concentrate our thoughts on you.
>
> When we listen to the reading of the Bible, help us to understand it, and to understand what it means for us.
>
> When we sing your praise, help us to sing because we really love you.

So help us tonight to worship you in spirit and in truth: through Jesus Christ our Lord.   Amen.

*The Reading Lesson:* Psalm 119.103-112

*Prayer*

O God, our Father, we thank you that you have made all things and made them well.

We thank you for the world in which we live.

> For the light of the day and the dark of the night;
>
> For the glory of the sunlight, for the silver splendour of the moon, and for the star-scattered sky;
>
> For the hills and the sea, for the busy city streets, for the open road and the wind on our faces:
>> We thank you, O God.

We thank you for ourselves.

> For hands to work, and eyes to see, and ears to hear;
>
> For minds to think, and memories to remember, and hearts to love:
>> We thank you, O God.

We thank you for all that makes life worthwhile.
> For a task to do, and for health of body, for accuracy of hand and eye;
> For skill of mind and brain to do it;
> For homes and for friends and for loved ones:
>> We thank you, O God.

We thank you that this life is not the end.
> That we are preparing ourselves for another and a greater life;
> That there is a place where all questions will be answered, and all hopes realized;
> That we will meet again those whom we have loved and lost awhile:
>> We thank you, O God.

We thank you most of all for Jesus, our Friend and our Example, our Saviour and our Lord.
Help us to try to deserve a little better all the gifts which you have given to us.

### A Prayer of William Bright

O God, by whom the meek are guided in judgment, and light riseth up in darkness for the godly; grant us in our doubts and uncertainties the grace to ask what thou wouldst have us to do; that the Spirit of wisdom may save us from all false choices, and that in thy light we may see the light, and in thy straight path may not stumble: through Jesus Christ our Lord. Amen.

### The Blessing

Lord, dismiss us with thy blessing, that we, inspired by this hour, may radiate light and life. Amen.

# THE FRUIT OF THE SPIRIT

*The Opening Prayer*

O God, we come to you tonight for your help and your blessing.

> Lord, what we know not, teach us;
> Lord, what we have not, give us;
> Lord, what we are not, make us.

Hear this our prayer, through Jesus Christ our Lord. Amen.

*(Prayers for Club and Hostel)*

*The Reading Lesson:* Galatians 5.16-23

*Prayer*

Let us ask God to give us the fruit of his Spirit in our lives.

O God, our Father, give us the fruit of your Spirit in our lives.

> Love, that we may love you as you have loved us, and that we may love our fellowmen as you love them;
>
> Joy, that we may be happy ourselves, and that we may help others to be happy;
>
> Peace, that we may never again be restless, and worried, and nervous:
>
> > Grant us these things, O God.
>
> Patience, that we may no longer be irritable and in too big a hurry;
>
> Kindness, that we may desire to give rather than to get, to share rather than to keep, to praise rather than to criticize, to forgive rather than to condemn;
>
> Goodness, that we may be an example and a help to all:
>
> > Grant us these things, O God.

Faithfulness, that through all the chances and the changes of life we may be true to ourselves, true to our loved ones, and true to you;

Gentleness, that we may be humble and not proud, and that we may never deliberately or carelessly hurt others;

Self-control, that no moment of impulse or of passion may make us to injure another or to bring shame on ourselves.

> Grant us these things, O God.

Help us so to live that on our lives there may be the reflection of the goodness of the Master, whose we are and whom we seek to serve.

### A Prayer of Alfred the Great

Lord God Almighty, I charge thee of thy great mercy and by the token of thy holy rood (cross) that thou guide me to thy will and to my soul's need better than I can myself, that above all things I may inwardly love thee with a clean mind and a clean body; for thou art my Maker, my Help and my Hope: through Jesus Christ our Lord. Amen.

### The Blessing

Now the God of peace, who brought again from the dead our Lord Jesus Christ, that great Shepherd of the sheep, make us perfect in every good work to do his will, working in us that which is well-pleasing in his sight, through Jesus Christ, to whom be glory for ever and ever. Amen.

# COURTESY

*The Opening Prayer*

Help us, O God, to accept the disciplines which you are wishing to lay upon us:

> The discipline of work and of study, that we may train and equip ourselves to do a good and useful day's work in the world;
>
> The discipline of prayer, that we may always live close to you;
>
> The discipline of service, that we may work for others and not for ourselves;
>
> The discipline of Christian living, that we may be true athletes and soldiers of our Master.

This we ask for your love's sake. Amen.

*The Reading Lesson:* John 17.15-26

*Prayer*

Help us, O God, always to live in courtesy towards everyone whom we meet.

Help us

> Never to speak an angry, an impatient, a boorish, an impolite or a discourteous word;
>
> Never to make people feel a nuisance;
>
> Never to do things so grudgingly and so unwillingly that it is worse than not doing them at all;
>
> Never to give anything in such a way that the gift becomes an insult;
>
> Never to treat people in such a way that it embarrasses them, or makes them feel small, or humiliates them.

Help us
>Always to be kind;
>Always to make people feel that they are welcome and that we care;
>Always to think of the feelings of others as much as we would wish them to think of ours;
>Always to respect and never to laugh at the things which are important and sacred to someone else.

Help us to walk looking unto Jesus, and to make him the pattern of our lives.

## An Ancient Prayer of the Church

Bless all who worship thee from the rising of the sun to the going down of the same. Of thy goodness, give us; with thy love, inspire us; by thy Spirit, guide us; by thy power, protect us; in thy mercy, receive us, now and always. Amen.

## The Blessing

Go forth into the world in peace; be of good courage; hold fast that which is good; render to no man evil for evil; strengthen the faint-hearted; support the weak; help the afflicted; honour all men; love and serve the Lord, rejoicing in the power of the Holy Spirit. And may the blessing of God Almighty, the Father, the Son and the Holy Spirit, be upon us and remain with us for ever. Amen.

# EQUIPMENT FOR LIFE

*The Opening Prayer*

O God, our Father, make us so eager to seek the truth that no study may be too difficult for us and no thinking too adventurous.

Make us so willing to serve you and our fellowmen that no task may be too wearisome for us and that no one may ever appeal in vain to us for help and sympathy.

Make us so to feel your love for us that our hearts may go out to you in wonder, love and praise.

This we ask for your love's sake. Amen.

*The Reading Lesson: Colossians* 3.23—4.5

*Prayer*

O God, we thank you for everything which widens our knowledge and which equips us more fully for the task of life and living.

For school and college and university;
For all wise teachers and instructors;
For those who teach not only by their words but also by their example:
> We thank you, O God.

For all good books;
For all that makes available for us the wisdom which has gone before;
For all the knowledge in the printed page with which we can store our mind:
> We thank you, O God.

For all the precious things the past has left us;
For great poetry to linger in the memory;

For great pictures and sculpture to delight the eye;
For great music to sound in the ear and to thrill the heart;
For all the heritage of beauty and loveliness into which we have entered:
> We thank you, O God.

For wireless and for television;
For all that brings the distant places to our own fireside;
For every opportunity to gain knowledge and wisdom;
For everything whereby we learn our profession, our trade, our craft;
And above all else for Jesus to show us how to use it all for your sake and for the sake of mankind:
> We give you thanks, O God.

## A Prayer of John Hunter

Grant, O Lord, that what we have said with our lips, we may believe in our hearts and practise in our lives; and of thy mercy keep us faithful to the end: for Christ's sake. Amen.

## The Blessing

May the blessing of God, Father, Son and Holy Spirit be upon us all now and stay with each one of us always. Amen.

# THAT WE MAY BE USEFUL

*The Opening Prayer*

Eternal God, whom to know is life eternal,
    help us daily to know you better, that daily we may
    have life more abundantly.
Eternal God, whom to serve is perfect freedom,
    help us daily to do your will, that in doing your will we
    may find our peace.
Eternal God, whom to love is fulness of joy,
    help us daily to love you more, that daily we may come
    nearer to loving you as you first loved us.
This we ask for your love's sake.   Amen.

*The Reading Lesson:* Luke 13.5-9

*Prayer*

Lord Jesus, who came not to be served but to serve, help us
to live useful lives.

   Help us always to encourage, and never to discourage
   others; always to be readier to praise than to criticize,
   and to sympathize rather than to condemn.

   Help us always to help, and never to hinder others.
   Help us always to make the work of others easier and
   not harder. Help us not to find fault with the efforts of
   others, unless we are prepared to try to do the thing
   better ourselves. Make us more ready to co-operate
   than to object, and more ready to say yes than to say
   no when anyone appeals to us for help.

   Help us always to be a good example, and never a bad
   example. Help us always to make it easier for others
   to do the right thing, and never to make it easier for

them to go wrong. Help us to remember that what is safe for us may be dangerous for others. Help us always to take our stand beside anyone who is standing for the right.

So grant that indeed our lives may be like lights in the world.

*A Prayer of St Augustine*

Watch thou, dear Lord, with those who wake, or watch, or weep tonight, and give thine angels charge over those who sleep. Tend thy sick ones, O Lord Christ. Rest thy weary ones. Bless thy dying ones. Soothe thy suffering ones. Pity thine afflicted ones. Shield thy joyous ones. And all for thy love's sake. Amen.

*The Blessing*

The grace of the Lord Jesus Christ be on us all and go with each one of us. Amen.

# THE USE OF OUR POSSESSIONS

*The Opening Prayer*

Rid us, O God, of the faults which spoil us, and defend us from the sins that beset us, that, forgiven by your love, protected by your power, and strengthened by your grace we may live in goodness and in purity all the days of our life: through Jesus Christ our Lord. Amen.

*The Reading Lesson:* I Timothy 6.1-11

*Prayer*

O God, you have given us all that we have. Teach us to use rightly our money and our material possessions.

Grant that we may never make money dishonestly or use it selfishly.

Keep us alike from being mean and miserly, and from being spendthrift and extravagant.

Help us to value independence and to have a horror of debt.

Help us always to fulfil our obligations to our parents and to our home, and never to grudge what we have to contribute to the common stock.

Make us always ready to give to the poor, the aged, and the needy, and to those who never have enough.

Help us to be generous to our church, so that through us your kingdom may be upbuilt, and your people helped and comforted, in this place, in this land, and in lands across the sea.

Help us always to remember that you love a cheerful giver, and that it is always a happier thing to give than to get.

*A Prayer of Lancelot Andrewes*

Take us, we pray thee, O Lord of our life, into thy keeping this night and for ever. O thou Light of lights, keep us from inward darkness; grant us to sleep in peace, that we may arise to work according to thy will: through Jesus Christ our Lord. Amen.

*The Blessing*

May grace, mercy and peace from Father, Son and Holy Spirit rest upon us all now and abide with each one of us for ever. Amen.

*The Opening Prayer*

Grant, O God, that we may never come to the end of any day without speaking to you and without listening to you speaking to us. And make us to feel you very near to us tonight as we end this day with you: through Jesus Christ our Lord.  Amen.

*The Reading Lesson:* Romans 6.1-14

*Prayer*

O Lord Jesus, help us to be true to our faith and true to you, when things are difficult.

When we have to stand alone;
When loyalty to you makes us unpopular with our fellowmen;
When doing the right thing involves us in the dislike or in the laughter of others:
    Help us still to be true.

Help us to be true to our faith and true to you, when it costs us something.

When our Christian duty demands more of our time than we really want to give;
When our Christian duty demands more of our money than we really want to give;
When our Christian duty demands more of an effort than we really want to make;
    Help us still to be true.

Help us to be true to our faith and true to you, when it is all against the things we instinctively want to do.

When we don't want to be unselfish;
When we have no desire to think of others;
When the last thing we want is to forgive someone who
  has injured us;
            Help us still to be true.

Give us strength to do what we cannot do and to be what
we cannot be; and help us to remember that by ourselves
we can do nothing but that with you all things are possible.

## A Prayer of Archbishop Laud

Grant, O God, that we may live in thy fear, die in thy
favour, rest in thy peace, rise in thy power, reign in thy
glory: for the sake of thy Son, Jesus Christ our Lord.
Amen.

## The Blessing

The peace of God sanctify us wholly, and may our whole
spirit and soul and body be preserved blameless unto the
coming of our Lord Jesus Christ. Amen.

# RESCUE FROM OUR FAULTS

*The Opening Prayer*

Grant, O God, that, remembering your holiness, we may come into your presence with penitence and godly fear.

Grant that, remembering your majesty, we may come into your presence with reverence and with humility.

Grant that, remembering your love, we may come into your presence with the trust and confidence of children who know that they are coming to a Father who, no matter what they have done, will not turn them away.   Amen.

*The Reading Lesson:* James 1.16-27

*Prayer*

O God, our Father, save us and rescue us from the faults to which we are so prone.

Keep us,

> From saying one thing with our words and another with our deeds;
>
> From criticizing others for that which we allow in ourselves;
>
> From demanding standards from others which we ourselves make no effort to fulfil.

Keep us,

> From flirting with temptation and from playing with fire;
>
> From the indecision that cannot say yes or no and be done with it;
>
> From the reluctance to break with habits which we know are wrong.

Keep us,

> From trying to make the best of both worlds, and from trying to please both men and you;
>
> From living one way on Sunday and another on Monday;
>
> From anything which would keep us from giving our whole loyalty, our whole allegiance, our whole life, and whole heart to you.

### A Great Prayer by an unknown Author

O Christ, our only Saviour, so dwell within us that we may go forth with the light of hope in our eyes, and the fire of inspiration on our lips, thy word on our tongue, and thy love in our hearts: through Jesus Christ our Lord. Amen.

### The Blessing

May grace, mercy and peace from Father, Son and Holy Spirit, one God, be on us all now and stay with each one of us always. Amen.

# THE GIFTS WE NEED

*The Opening Prayer*

O God, our Father, we have come to you tonight to find the strength and the beauty for life which we do not possess, and which can only come from you. Give us this night the gifts for which we pray: through Jesus Christ our Lord. Amen.

*The Reading Lesson:* Proverbs 2.1-15

*Prayer*

O God, give us the gifts which we need most of all.

Wisdom always to choose the right, and courage always to do it;

Strength to overcome temptation, and prudence ever to stay in the straight way;

Clear sight to see what to do, and perseverance never to give up trying to do it:

Grant us these things, O God.

Diligence in study, and fidelity in work;

Purity in pleasure, and delight in simple things;

Honour in every action, and truth in every word:

Grant us these things, O God.

Loyalty to our friends, and forgiveness to our enemies;

Sympathy for all in sorrow, help for all in need, understanding for those who have made mistakes;

Love for our fellowmen, and love for you:

Grant us these things, O God.

*A Prayer from* The Penitent Pilgrim *written in 1641*

Gracious Lord, in whom are laid up all the treasures of

knowledge and wisdom, direct us in the ways of life, remove from us the ways of death. Give us a soft and meek spirit, that we may help the succourless, and comfort the comfortless. O our Lord, pardon us for the neglect of this duty, and make us to redeem the time with a cheerful constancy. Amen.

*The Blessing*

The grace of the Lord Jesus Christ be with us all. Amen

# FOR THOSE TO WHOM WE
# OWE SO MUCH

*The Opening Prayer*

Help us, O God, so to meet you tonight that we may go out knowing you better, loving you more, and to serve you more faithfully: through Jesus Christ our Lord. Amen.

*The Reading Lesson:* I John 4.7-12

*Prayer*

O God, our Father, we thank you for all the people you have given to us to whom we owe more than we can ever repay.

> For those who are an example to us, and who have shown us what life should be;
> For those who are an inspiration to us, and who fill us with the desire and the determination to do better;
> For those whose judgment we respect, and to whom we know that we can go for guidance and for advice;
> For those who, we know, will understand, even if we have to tell them of some foolish mistake that we have made or some bad thing that we have done;
> For those to whom we are not ashamed or afraid to go and ask for help:
> > We thank you, O God.

> For those who help us,
> > To bear our sorrows;
> > To solve our problems;
> > To conquer our temptations;
> > To live more nearly as we ought;
> > And above all else for Jesus Christ,

The pattern of our lives and the Saviour of our souls:
We thank you, O God.

## An Ancient Prayer

Help us, O Lord, always to wait for thee, to wish for thee, and to watch for thee, that at thy coming again thou mayest find us ready: for thy sake we ask it. Amen.

## The Blessing

The love of God, the grace of our Lord Jesus Christ, the fellowship of the Holy Spirit be with us all now and stay with each one of us always. Amen.

# REMEMBERING OUR
# RESPONSIBILITIES

*The Opening Prayer*

O God, our Father, speak to us tonight that here in your presence we may find knowledge of what you want us to do and strength to do it: through Jesus Christ our Lord. Amen.

*The Reading Lesson:* Galatians 5.16—6.2

*Prayer*

O God, Lord of all good life, give us in all things a true sense of responsibility.

Help us at all times to remember our responsibility to ourselves.

Help us,

> Never to act in such a way that we shall lose our self-respect;
>
> Never to let ourselves down by doing something which is mean and low, disloyal and dishonourable;
>
> Never to do anything which we would afterwards regret, perhaps spend the rest of our life regretting.

Help us at all times to remember our responsibility to our friends, and to those whom we love, and who love us.

Help us,

> Never to disappoint those who love us;
>
> Never to fail those who trust us;
>
> Never to bring grief or heartbreak to those in whose hearts we have a special place.

Help us at all times to remember our responsibility to our fellowmen.

Help us,

> Not to be the kind of people who are always remembering their rights and always forgetting their duties;
>
> Not to be the kind of people who want to get everything out of life and to put nothing into it;
>
> Not to be the kind of people who do not care what happens to others so long as they are all right.

Help us at all times to remember our responsibility to you.
Help us,

> To remember that we shall answer to you for the way we have used the gifts you gave us;
>
> To remember that we shall give account for all that we have been allotted in this life;
>
> To remember at all times how you have loved us and how Jesus died for us.

## An Ancient Prayer

Thine is the day, O Lord, and thine is the night. Grant that the Sun of Righteousness may abide in our hearts to drive away the darkness of evil thoughts: through Jesus Christ our Lord. Amen.

## The Blessing

The grace of the Lord Jesus Christ be with us all. Amen.

# FOR TRUE AMBITION

*The Opening Prayer*

Lord Jesus, you have promised to be there wherever your people come to meet with you. Help us to feel you very near tonight. Help us to hear your voice speaking to us when your word is read. And help us, when we pray, not only to speak to you, but also to listen to you speaking to us. This we ask for your love's sake. Amen.

*The Reading Lesson:* Mark 10.35-45

*Prayer*

O God, our Creator and our Father, it is you who gave us life. Now teach us how to use life.

When we are thinking and planning what to do with life, help us to have the right kind of ambition.

Help us to think

Not of how much we can get out of life, but of how much we can put into life;

Not of how much we can get, but of how much we can give;

Not of the number of people we can use, but of the number of people to whom we can be of use.

Help us to think

Of money, not as something to spend on ourselves, but as something to share with others;

Of leisure time, not as something always to be used on pleasure, but as something which can be used to help the Church, this fellowship and the community in which we live;

Of work, not as a grim and stern necessity, but as that which makes life worthwhile, and help us to work, not for ourselves, and not for a master, but always for you and in the service of our fellowmen.

Jesus was in the world as one who loved his fellowmen and as one who served.

Help us always to be like him, that in his service we may find our perfect freedom and in doing his will our peace. This we ask for your love's sake. Amen.

## St Francis' Prayer

Lord, make us instruments of thy peace.
Where there is hatred, let us sow love;
Where there is injury, pardon;
Where there is discord, union;
Where there is doubt, faith;
Where there is despair, hope;
Where there is darkness, light;
Where there is sadness, joy;
for thy mercy and thy truth's sake. Amen.

## The Ascription and the Blessing

Now unto him that is able to keep us from falling, and to present us faultless before the presence of his glory with exceeding joy, to the only wise God, our Saviour, be glory and majesty, dominion and power, both now and ever. And may the blessing of God, Father, Son and Holy Spirit, be on us all now and stay with each one of us always. Amen.

# THE LAND IN WHICH WE LIVE

*The Opening Prayer*

O God, send out your light and your truth upon us tonight, so that we may have light upon our problems, and so that we may know what we ought to do and where we ought to go. And make us always willing to accept your guidance so that we may make no mistakes and so that we may have nothing to regret: through Jesus Christ our Lord. Amen.

*The Reading Lesson:* Psalm 122

*Prayer*

O God, our Father, we thank you that you have made us citizens of this land in which we live.

For freedom to worship you as our conscience commands us;

For our freedom to speak our mind without fear;

For the liberty, the just laws, and the good government which we enjoy;

For all those who lived and died to win this freedom for us;
We thank you, O God.

For everything which the state does for us;

For opportunities of education in school and college and university;

For all that is done for the aged and for the sick and the poor and for those who have no work to do;

For the standards of living which we enjoy;
We thank you, O God.

Bless those who rule and govern and administer our country:
The Prime Minister and all the ministers of state;
All members of Parliament;

Those in the Civil Service;
Those who serve on the Councils of the cities and the towns, the counties and the districts;
Those engaged in any kind of public service:
Bless them all.

Grant that this country may have leaders who are themselves led by you, and who are men and women who are not out for prestige but for service, and who set the good of the community above the good of any class or party.

Help us in our time to be good citizens of this land. Help us

To be diligent at school so that we may fit ourselves for the work that one day we will do;

To train ourselves in a trade, a craft, a profession, a vocation that we may one day be useful members of the community;

To develop a sense of responsibility so that we may never be the kind of people who leave all work and service to others.

While we think of our own land, we also pray for other lands. Help us to work and pray to help you to send

Freedom to lands where men are oppressed;
Food and health to lands where men are hungry and sick;
The story of Jesus to lands where men have never heard of him.

Help us to be worthy of the heritage into which we have entered, and to pass it on an even finer thing to those who follow after. This we ask for Jesus' sake.   Amen.

*The Sarum Primer Prayer*

God be in my head, and in my understanding;
God be in my eyes, and in my looking;
God be in my mouth, and in my speaking;
God be in my heart, and in my thinking;
God be at mine end, and at my departing.

*The Blessing*

The grace of the Lord Jesus Christ be with us all.   Amen.

# THE LIFE WE LIVE

*The Opening Prayer*

O God, we have come to you tonight,
>To thank you for all your gifts;
>To ask your forgiveness for all our sins;
>To receive your guidance for all our actions.

Hear us; forgive us; and direct us: for your love's sake. Amen.

*The Reading Lesson:* Romans 12.9-21

*Prayer*

We thank you, O God, for all the interesting things in life.
>For music and for rhythm;
>For pictures and for plays;
>For wireless and for television;
>For the things which make us laugh;
>For the things which command our interest;
>For the things which widen our knowledge:
>>We thank you, O God.

>For our work and for our study;
>And for the real satisfaction of a difficult task mastered, completed and done:
>>We thank you, O God.

O God, forgive us for the things in us which have spoiled life.
>If we have been lazy at work;
>If we have been difficult to get on with at school, at our work, or in this fellowship;
>If we have been inconsiderate and ungrateful at home;
>If we have been forgetful of you:
>>Forgive us, O God.

O God, we thank you for all the possibilities of life. Help us,

    To work so hard;

    To study so diligently;

    To discipline ourselves so firmly,

that we may turn the possibilities into realities and so make all our plans and dreams come true. So grant that we may ever be,

    A credit to ourselves;

    A help to others;

    A joy to you.

Bless our friends and our comrades and our loved ones. Bless all those in trouble of any kind; and bless each one of us.

*St Patrick's Prayer*

        Christ be with me, Christ within me,
        Christ before me, Christ beside me.
           Christ to win me,
        Christ to comfort and restore me,
        Christ beneath me, Christ above me,
        Christ in quiet, Christ in danger,
        Christ in hearts of all that love me,
        Christ in mouth of friend and stranger.

*The Blessing*

The grace of the Lord Jesus Christ be with us all.  Amen.

*The Opening Prayer*

O God, our Father, the darkness and the light are both alike to you. All through today you have kept us in our going out and in our coming in. Bless us now as evening comes and as the long day closes, and be with us as we end this day with you: through Jesus Christ our Lord. Amen.

*The Reading Lesson:* Psalm 139.1-12

*Prayer*

O God, help us always to be good members of this fellowship.

Help us,

> To argue without losing our temper;
> To play games without being too eager to win at any cost;
> To welcome the stranger;
> To see that the shy are not left out of things;
> To take our due share of the tasks that have to be done, the washing up, the clearing away, the routine duties without which our activities cannot go on;
> To support our leaders loyally, and to accept the discipline and the obedience which membership of this fellowship brings with it.

Help us to live in the world all that we learn here. So help us to be,

> More diligent in study;
> More conscientious in work;
> More grateful and considerate at home;
> More reverent at worship and in church.

Bless those who are in sickness, in sorrow and in trouble. Bring back those who have drifted away from our fellowship, and help us to go to them and to try to persuade them to come back. Bless all those whose hearts are sad, whose lives are lonely, whose minds are perplexed, and whose bodies are in pain.

Bless our friends, our comrades and our loved ones; and bless each one of us.

### St Richard of Chichester's Prayer

> Thanks be to thee, my Lord Jesus Christ,
> > For all the benefits thou hast won for me,
> > For all the pains and insults thou hast borne for me.
> O most merciful Redeemer, Friend, and Brother,
> > May I know thee more clearly,
> > Love thee more dearly,
> > And follow thee more nearly:
> > > For ever and ever.  Amen.

### The Blessing

The Lord bless us and keep us: the Lord make his face to shine upon us, and be gracious unto us: the Lord lift up his countenance upon us, and give us peace.  Amen.

*The Opening Prayer*

O God, who made both night and day, we thank you for taking care of us all through today, and for bringing us in safety to this evening hour; and now we have come to ask your blessing before the night comes, and before we go home to sleep. Be with us now as we think of you: through Jesus Christ our Lord. Amen.

*The Reading Lesson:* Psalm 145.9-18

*Prayer*

O God, our Father, we thank you for everything which keeps us right when we are tempted to go wrong.

For those who set us a good example;
For those who give us good advice, and kindly rebuke, when we need it;
For the friends who make us want to be better than we are;
For those who love us and who believe in us and whom we could not bear to disappoint:
We thank you, O God.

For the voice of conscience to warn us when to stop;
For the traditions which we cannot let down;
For the fellowship of this club;
For the memory that you see us:
We give you thanks, O God.

O God, forgive us for the times when we went wrong.
For times when we knew the right thing and did the wrong thing;

For things that now we wish that we had never said and
done;
For anything which makes us ashamed when we think
about it:
Forgive us, O God.

O God, bless those who this night are on journeys on the
roads, the railways, in the air, and at sea; and bless those
who must work while others sleep.
Bless those who are ill, especially those in hospitals and in
infirmaries. Bless those who have lost loved ones and who
are sad. Bless those who are in prison and in disgrace.
Bless our friends without whom life would not be the same.
Bless our club and our work, our play and our study
within it.
Go with us to our homes and guard us while we sleep, and
wake us refreshed for work tomorrow.

*St Benedict's Prayer*

O gracious and holy Father, give us
Wisdom to perceive thee;
Intelligence to understand thee;
Diligence to seek thee;
Patience to wait for thee;
Eyes to behold thee;
A heart to meditate upon thee;
And a life to proclaim thee:
through the power of the Spirit of Jesus Christ our Lord.
Amen.

*The Blessing*

May grace and mercy and peace from Father, Son and Holy
Spirit, one God, rest on us now and stay with each one of us
this night and always. Amen.

*The Opening Prayer*

O God, you have given us the day to work and the night to rest. Be with us for this brief time before we go home, while we think of you and of your word, and help us for these few minutes to feel you very near: through Jesus Christ our Lord. Amen.

*The Reading Lesson:* Philippians 4.4-13

*Prayer*

O God, thank you for today and thank you specially for this club and for everything in it that we enjoy so much.

> For the games we have played;
> For the discussions and the arguments in which we have taken part;
> For the things we have learned;
> For the people we have met and the friends we have made:
>> We thank you, O God.

O God, forgive us for all the wrong things which we have done and been.

> If by our bad temper or by our stubbornness we have done anything to spoil the fellowship of this club;
> If in our laziness and in our selfishness we have wanted everything done for us and have done nothing ourselves to help;
> If we have criticized the efforts of others while we were not prepared to do anything ourselves:
>> Forgive us, O God.

O God, bless those who specially need your help,
    Those who are ill and in pain;
    Those who are sad and in sorrow;
    Those who are strangers and in loneliness;
    Those who are tempted and in danger;
    Those who have been foolish and who are in trouble:
Bless this club, and specially bless those who give their
time and their thought and their work to make it what it is.
Bless all those we love and all who love us. And help us to
sleep well tonight and to work well tomorrow.

*Ignatius Loyola's Prayer*

Teach us, good Lord, to serve thee as thou deservest;
    To give and not to count the cost;
    To fight and not to heed the wounds;
    To toil and not to seek for rest;
    To labour, and to ask for no reward,
save that of knowing that we do thy will: through Jesus
Christ our Lord.   Amen.

# OUR CONFESSION, OUR THANKS-GIVING, OUR PETITION, OUR INTERCESSION

*The Opening Prayer*

This night, O God, we bring to you
> Our sorrow for our wrong-doing;
> Our gratitude for your gifts;
> Our requests for our needs;
> Our remembrance of others,

in the sure certainty that you will hear them all.  Amen.

*The Reading Lesson:* Romans 8.31-39

As at evening-time we look back across today, let us begin by asking for God's forgiveness.

> If we have failed our friends today;
> If we have disappointed or hurt those who love us;
> If we have shamed or disgraced ourselves;
> If we have grieved you :
>> Forgive us, O God.

Let us be silent, and in the silence let each one of us ask God's forgiveness for anything for which we are specially sorry.

Now let us give God thanks.

> For time that we have spent with our friends and with those we love;
> For times when we talked and times when we laughed together today;
> If, as today closes, we feel that we are closer to one another, and nearer to you,
>> We thank you, O God.

118

Let us be silent, and in the silence let each one of us thank God for anything for which we are specially grateful.

Now let us ask God for the things we need to live well.

> Courage always to do the right;
> Strength always to resist the wrong;
> Perseverance never to give up;
> Respect for ourselves and love for all others:
> > Grant us these things, O God.

Let us be silent, and in the silence let each one of us ask God for anything which we know that we specially need.

Now let us pray for others.

> O God, our Father,
> Heal the sick,
> Comfort the sad,
> Be with the lonely,
> Cheer the disappointed,
> Bless and keep specially those who are far from home.

Let us be silent, and in the silence let each one of us name before God those we love most of all, especially our absent friends.

### Dr Johnson's Prayer

Make us remember, O God, that every day is thy gift, and ought to be used according to thy command: through Jesus Christ our Lord. Amen.

### The Blessing

Go in peace; God the Father, Son and Holy Spirit, bless, preserve and keep us this night and for evermore. Amen.

# EVERY PART OF LIFE

*The Opening Prayer*

O God, we have come to you tonight because we want,
>To know you better with our minds;
>To love you better with our hearts;
>To serve you better with our lives.

We ask you to widen our knowledge, to deepen our love, and to strengthen our service: through Jesus Christ our Lord. Amen.


*The Reading Lesson:* Ephesians 6.10-18


*Prayer*

O God, you gave us life, help us to live each part of our lives as we ought.

At home
>make us good sons and daughters in whom our parents will never be grieved or disappointed.

At school and college and university
>make us diligent and conscientious, always remembering that we must bear the yoke in our youth, if we are to make our life useful to others and honourable to ourselves.

At work
>make us faithful and reliable, always putting our best into it, workers who have no need to be ashamed.

In our games
>help us to play hard, but to play fair, to win without boasting and to lose without making excuses.

At our pleasure
>help us never to find delight in anything which would hurt ourselves or others, or in things which we would desire to hide, or in things which some day we would bitterly regret.

In our fellowship here
>make us friendly and loyal in its activities, always willing to take our share in its duties, and always reverent in its worship.

*Sir Francis Drake's Prayer*

O Lord God, when thou givest to thy servants to endeavour any great matter, grant us also to know that it is not the beginning, but the continuing of the same unto the end, until it be thoroughly finished, which yieldeth the true glory: through him who for the finishing of thy work laid down his life, our Redeemer, Jesus Christ. Amen.

*The Blessing*

The peace of God, which passeth all understanding, keep our hearts and minds in the knowledge of God and of his Son Jesus Christ our Lord; and the blessing of God Almighty, the Father, the Son and the Holy Spirit be amongst us and remain with us always. Amen.

# TO LIVE AS WE OUGHT

*A Prayer of George Adam Smith for use before reading the Bible*

Almighty and most merciful God, who hast given the Bible to be the revelation of thy great love to man, and of thy power and will to save him; grant that our study of it may not be made vain by the callousness or carelessness of our hearts, but that by it we may be confirmed in penitence, lifted to hope, made strong for service, and above all filled with the true knowledge of thee and of thy Son Jesus Christ. Amen.

*The Reading Lesson:* 1 Timothy 6.3-16

*Prayer*

O God, tomorrow we go back to the world and to all its work and its activities. We remember that Jesus prayed, not that his friends should be taken out of the world, but that they should be kept from the evil of the world. Help us to live in this world as we ought to live.

Help us

To do the world's work faithfully and well;

To enjoy the world's pleasures wisely and temperately;

To value the world's goods, without becoming enslaved by them and without despising them;

To resist the world's temptations bravely and resolutely;

Always to remember that the greatest importance of the world is that it is the school and the training-ground for the still greater life which some day we shall live.

Help us to live in the world, not as those whose interests never look beyond the horizons of the world, but as those who always remember that in you we live and move and have our being, and that we are pledged to follow in the footsteps of our Lord and Master Jesus Christ.

*A Prayer of Robert Louis Stevenson*

Give us courage and gaiety and the quiet mind. Spare us to our friends, soften us to our enemies. Bless us, if it may be, in all our innocent endeavours. If it may not, give us strength to encounter that which is to come, that we may be brave in peril, constant in tribulation, temperate in wrath, and in all changes of fortune, and, down even to the gates of death, loyal and loving to one another: through Jesus Christ our Lord.   Amen.

*The Blessing*

The Lord preserve our going out and our coming in, from this time forth for evermore.   Amen.

*The Opening Prayer*

Give us this night, O God,
> The hearing ear;
> The understanding mind;
> The resolute will,

that we may be,
> Willing to listen to your word;
> Able to grasp its meaning for us;
> And strong to do it throughout the days of the
> week:

through Jesus Christ our Lord.   Amen.

*The Reading Lesson:* John 3.1-17

*Prayer*

Let us tonight pray not only for ourselves but for the whole
world which God so loved.

O God, send peace upon earth, that the nations no longer
may prepare for war, and that they may try, not to
destroy, but to understand each other.

O God, bless those parts of the world where men are learning the meaning of freedom and of liberty, and where
new nations are being born. Take away all bitterness
and hatred, and grant that men of all colours and races
may learn to live in fellowship together.

O God, bless those places in the world where the name of
Jesus is not known, or where it is rejected. Strengthen
and uphold all missionaries in the peril and the loneli-
ness of their task; and bring quickly the day when all
men everywhere will confess that Jesus Christ is Lord.

O God, bless those parts of the world where people are
homeless and hungry, and grant that those of us who

have may ever be ready to share their plenty with those who have too little.

O God, bless those nations who have a different political creed and a different way of life from ours; and save us from being too quick to condemn that which we do not understand just because it is different, and help all men everywhere to find a fellowship in Jesus Christ which will cross all creeds and frontiers and weld them into one.

And help us to work, and to pray, and to give, and to sacrifice to bring the day when the kingdoms of the world will be the Kingdom of the Lord: through Jesus Christ our Lord. Amen.

### The Prayer of the House of Commons

(This prayer is used at every sitting of the House of Commons. It was originally composed by Sir Christopher Yelverton, MP for Northampton, about the year 1578.)

Almighty God, by whom kings reign and princes decree justice, and from whom alone cometh all counsel, wisdom and understanding. We, thine unworthy servants, here gathered together in thy name, do most humbly beseech thee to send down the heavenly wisdom from above, to direct and guide us in all our consultations.

And grant that we, having thy fear always before our eyes, and laying aside all private interests, prejudices and partial affections, the result of all our counsels may be the glory of thy blessed name, the maintenance of true religion and justice, the safety, honour, and happiness of the Queen, the public welfare, peace and tranquillity of the realm, and the uniting and knitting together of the hearts of all persons and estates within the same in true Christian love and charity towards one another: through Jesus Christ our Lord and Saviour. Amen.

### The Blessing

May the God of all grace, who has called us into his eternal glory by Christ Jesus, make us perfect, stablish, strengthen, settle us; to whom be glory and dominion for ever and ever. Amen.

# THE WAY TO TRUE WEALTH

*The Opening Prayer*

O God,

> You are King; help us to come to you in loyal allegiance;
>
> You are Judge; help us to come to you in heartfelt sorrow for the wrong that we have done;
>
> You are Father; help us to come to you in confident and loving trust;
>
> You are God; help us to come to you in humble reverence and adoration.

Hear this our prayer: through Jesus Christ our Lord. Amen.

*The Reading Lesson:* Luke 12.13-21

*Prayer*

Help us, O God, to set our hearts only on the things which make life truly rich;

> Knowledge and skill which will make us able to make a real contribution to the world's work;
>
> Character which will make everyone able to trust us and to rely on us;
>
> Friends who will always be true to us.

To that end give us

> The diligence which will never shirk the toil of learning;
>
> The discipline which will make us refuse the easy way in order to train ourselves in goodness;
>
> The loyalty which will never let anyone down.

Forgive us
>    If we have been lazy in learning and far slower than we
>    need have been;
>    If we have been careless in living and far more self-
>    indulgent than we should have been;
>    If we have been disloyal in friendship and far less faith-
>    ful than we should have been.

Help us from now on
>    To use to the full every gift and talent you have given
>    us;
>    To overcome every weakness which has us in its grip;
>    To be forever true to you and to our friends and loved
>    ones, no matter what the cost.

*A Prayer of St Thomas Aquinas*

God of all goodness, grant unto us to desire ardently, to
seek wisely, to know surely, and to accomplish perfectly thy
holy will, for the glory of thy name.   Amen.

*The Blessing*

The grace of the Lord Jesus Christ go with us all.   Amen.

# THAT WE MAY BE AN EXAMPLE
## TO ALL

*The Opening Prayer*

O God, our Father, bless us as we come to you this night.

> As pilgrims on the way we come to you for guidance for our road;

> As soldiers of the King we come to you for strength for the battle;

> As disciples of the Master we come to you for knowledge in our ignorance;

> As ambassadors of Christ we come to you for grace to make us good advertisements for our faith and for our Church.

This night we look to you for help for every need: through Jesus Christ our Lord. Amen.

*The Reading Lesson:* Matthew 7.13-20

*Prayer*

Help us, O God, to rid ourselves of all the things which keep us from being good examples of the faith which we profess.

Help us

> Never to demand standards from others which we never even attempt to live up to ourselves;

> Never to contradict with our lives that which we say with our lips;

> Never to be one thing to people's face and another behind their back.

Help us

> Never to make a promise and then to break it because it is difficult to keep;
>
> Never to do anything dishonourable, either to avoid trouble or to make gain;
>
> Never to be disloyal to a friend or untrue to a loved one.

Help us

> Never to teach or to persuade anyone to do a wrong thing;
>
> Never to give an example which will make it easier for someone else to go wrong;
>
> Never to laugh at anyone else's beliefs, and never to hide our own.

Help us to live that we shall never bring disgrace to ourselves, heartbreak to others, or grief to you.

## An Ancient Prayer from the Gregorian Sacramentary

Go before us, O Lord, in all our doings with thy most gracious favour, and further us with thy continual help; that in all our works, begun, continued, and ended in thee, we may glorify thy holy name, and finally by thy mercy obtain everlasting life: through Jesus Christ our Lord. Amen.

## The Blessing

The grace of the Lord Jesus Christ, the love of God, the fellowship of the Holy Spirit be upon us and upon all whom we love here and everywhere, and stay with each one of us and them this night and always. Amen.

# FOR THOSE IN DISTRESS

*The Opening Prayer*

O God, our Father, as we worship you this night, make us
Humble enough to know that we need you;
Wise enough to understand what you will say to us;
Obedient enough to go out and to obey your commands: through Jesus Christ our Lord. Amen.

*The Reading Lesson:* Luke 4.33-40

*Prayer*

Lord Jesus, when you were on earth, they brought the sick to you and you healed them all. This night we ask you to bless all those in sickness, in weakness and in pain.

Those who are blind and who cannot see the light of the sun, the beauty of the world, or the faces of their friends;

Those who are deaf and who cannot hear the voices which speak to them;

Those who are helpless and who must lie in bed while others go out and in:
Bless all such.

Those whose minds have lost their reason;

Those who are so nervous that they cannot cope with life;

Those who worry about everything:
Bless all such.

Those who must face life under some handicap;

Those whose weakness means that they must always be careful;

Those who are lame and maimed and who cannot enter
into any of the strenuous activities or pleasures of life;
Those who have been crippled by accident, or by illness,
or who were born with a weakness of body or mind;
Bless all such.

Grant that we in our health and our strength may never find
those who are weak and handicapped a nuisance, but grant
that we may always do and give all that we can to help
them, and to make life easier for them.

*An Ancient Prayer from the Gelasian Sacramentary*

Lord God, Light of the minds that know thee, Life of the
souls that love thee, Strength of the thoughts that seek thee;
help us so to know thee that we may truly love thee, and so
to love thee that we may fully serve thee, whose service is
perfect freedom: through Jesus Christ our Lord. Amen.

*The Blessing*

God Almighty bless us with his Holy Spirit: guard us in
our going out and coming in; keep us ever steadfast in his
faith, free from sin, and safe from danger: through Jesus
Christ our Lord. Amen.

# IN TEMPTATION

*The Opening Prayer*

Give us this night, O God, as we worship you,

> Your truth to tell us what we ought to believe and what we ought to do;
>
> Your strength to make us able to face the things which by ourselves we cannot do;
>
> Your love that we may love you as you have first loved us, and that we may love our fellowmen as you love them:

Through Jesus Christ our Lord. Amen.

*The Reading Lesson:* Luke 4.1-13

*Prayer*

Lord Jesus, you were tempted; help us when we are tempted.

When we are tempted, help us,

> Always to remember those who love us and trust us and believe in us, and whose hearts would be broken if we brought disgrace upon ourselves;
>
> Never to do anything which would bring us regret, remorse and shame to follow it;
>
> Never to do anything which we would have to hide, and about which we should be ashamed that others should know;
>
> Never to do anything which would injure anyone else;
>
> Always to remember that whatever we say or do you hear and see it.

Save us from ever being carried away by the heat or the impulse or the passion of the moment, and so forgetting the consequences of the thing we do.

Help us never to disobey our conscience and never to do anything which would take away our own self-respect.

Help us to make

> Our pleasure such that we would never wish to hide it;
> Our work such that we never need to be ashamed of it;
> Our conduct to others such that we will never regret it.

At all times keep

> Our thoughts pure and our words true;
> Our actions honourable and our bodies clean.

Help us so to live that we can take everything in life and show it to you.

### An Ancient Prayer

O heavenly Father, in whom we live and move and have our being, we humbly pray thee so to govern and guide us by thy Holy Spirit, that in all the cares and occupations of our daily life we may never forget thee, but remember that we are ever walking in thy sight: through Jesus Christ our Lord. Amen.

### The Blessing

From the rising of the sun to the going down of the same, of thy goodness give us, with thy love inspire us, by thy Spirit guide us, by thy power protect us, and in thy mercy receive us, now and ever. Amen.

# THE GOLDEN RULE

*The Opening Prayer*

Be with us, O God, tonight as we worship you,
> To teach us what we ought to know;
> To tell us what we ought to do;
> To make us what we ought to be.

This we ask for your love's sake.  Amen.

*The Reading Lesson:* Matthew 7.1-13

*Prayer*

Help us, O God, at all times to act towards others as we would wish them to act towards us.

Help us,
> To make the same allowances for others as we would wish them to make for us;
> To be as sympathetic and understanding to others as we would wish them to be to us;
> To encourage others as we would wish them to encourage us;
> To help others as we would wish them to help us;
> To be as just and fair to others as we would wish them to be to us;
> To forgive others as we would wish them to forgive us.

Before we criticize others, help us to remember what it feels like to be criticized.

Before we find fault with others, help us to remember what it feels like to be found fault with.

Before we condemn others, help us to remember what it feels like to be condemned.

134

Help us at all times to be like Jesus,
> Who went about doing good;
> Who was among men as one who serves;
> Who even on the Cross prayed that his enemies
> should be forgiven.

### An Evening Prayer from the Book of Common Prayer

Lighten our darkness, we beseech thee, O Lord; and by thy great mercy defend us from all perils and dangers of this night: for the love of thy only Son, our Saviour, Jesus Christ. Amen.

### The Blessing

May the blessing of God Almighty, the Father, the Son and the Holy Spirit, rest upon us and upon all our work and worship done in his name. May he give us light to guide us, courage to support us, and love to unite us, now and for evermore. Amen.

*The Opening Prayer*

Lord Jesus, Light of the World, give us your light tonight;
    Light to help us to see the truth;
    Light to help us to see the way we ought to go;
    Light to see ourselves as we are;
    Light to see you in all your majesty and your love.
This we ask through Jesus Christ our Lord. Amen.

*The Reading Lesson:* Psalm 8

*Prayer*

O God, our Father, tonight we ask you to bless those whom we love and those who are specially dear to us.

Bless our parents, and help us to live in such a way that we may never bring anxiety or sorrow to them.

Bless our friends, and help us to live in such a way that we may never fail them and never let them down.

Bless those whom we love, and help us to live in such a way that we may never be untrue, unfaithful or disloyal to them.

Bless those whom we love and from whom we are separated, those whom work and duty have taken to other towns and other countries, and to sea, and at all times keep us true to them and keep them true to us, and grant that distance may never make us forget them, until we and they meet again.

Bless those who are,
        Ill and in pain;
        Sad and in loneliness;
        Poor and in need;

Worried and in distress;
Discouraged and in despair;
Tempted and in danger.

Bless all missionaries and especially those who bring the messages of your love to lands where there are strife and tension because new nations are being born.

## A Prayer of Christina Rossetti

O Lord God of time and eternity, who makest us creatures of time that, when time is over, we may attain thy blessed eternity; with time, thy gift, give us also wisdom to redeem the time, lest our hour of grace be lost: for our Lord Jesus' sake. Amen.

## The Blessing

The grace of the Lord Jesus Christ be on us all now, and stay with each one of us always. Amen.

# FOR VICTORY OVER TEMPTATION

*The Opening Prayer*

Give us tonight, O God,
> Humility to listen to your word,
> Wisdom to understand your word;
> Obedience to attempt your word;
> Strength to obey your word:

through Jesus Christ our Lord who is the Word. Amen.

*The Reading Lesson:* Luke 9.57-62

*Prayer*

O God, our Father, give us strength to defeat the temptations which so often attack us.

> Help us in spite of all seductions to sin to keep our bodies chaste and pure.
>
> Help us in spite of all inducements to pride to keep our minds humble and ever learning.
>
> Help us in spite of all the invitations to give them to the wrong things to give our hearts only to the things which are honourable, and above all to you.

Keep us,

> From the self-indulgence and the lack of self-control which can ruin life for ourselves and for others;
>
> From the mental lethargy and laziness which will not make the effort to learn;
>
> From all wrong desires and all mistaken loyalties which will make us give our hearts to the wrong things.

And help us to love you so much that we will hate the sins which grieve you.

## A Prayer of John Baillie

Give me an open ear, O God, that I may hear thy voice calling me to high endeavour. Too often have I been deaf to the appeals thou hast addressed to me, but now give me courage to answer, Here am I, send me. And when any one of thy children, my human brothers, cries out in need, give me an open ear to hear in that cry thy call to service. Amen.

## The Blessing

The peace of God which passeth all understanding, keep our hearts and minds in the knowledge and love of God, and of his Son Jesus Christ our Lord, and the blessing of God Almighty, the Father, the Son and the Holy Spirit, be amongst us and remain with us always. Amen.

# FOR THE HELP OF GOD

*The Opening Prayer*

Give us this night, O God,

The gratitude which really wants to thank you;

The penitence which really wishes to tell you that it is sorry;

The sense of need which really makes us come to you for the things which you alone can give;

The obedience which will really make us listen and obey.

Hear and answer this our prayer, through Jesus Christ our Lord. Amen.

*The Reading Lesson:* Matthew 7.21-28

*Prayer*

O God, our Father, we ask your help so to live that we shall always be on the right way.

Guide us in every choice which life brings to us,

so that we may always choose the right way.

Purify all our ambitions,

so that we may set our hearts only on the things which please you.

Control all our thoughts,

that they may never linger on the wrong things, or stray down the pathways in which they ought not to go.

Guard our lips,

so that no word which would shame ourselves or hurt another may ever pass through them.

Direct our actions, so that we may always work with
diligence, act in honour, and live in kindness.

And help us not only to ask for your help but also always
to be willing to accept it when you offer it to us, so that we
may stop wanting our own way and begin to take yours.

## A Prayer of John Knox

Let thy mighty hand, O Lord our God, and outstretched
arm be our defence; thy mercy and loving kindness in Jesus
Christ, thy dear Son, our salvation; thy all-true word, our
instruction; the grace of thy life-giving Spirit our comfort
and consolation, to the end and in the end. Amen.

## The Closing Prayer

Lord Jesus, teach us to love thee and to abide with thee in
the love of the Father and the fellowship of the Holy Spirit,
now and ever. Amen.

# PENITENCE, PETITION, AND GRATITUDE

*The Opening Prayer*

Help us, O God, not to grudge these few minutes when we
worship you.

Help us not to regard them as just a formality which ends
our meeting.

Help us tonight really to listen for your voice, and really to
speak to you, so that we may go out to make life better
than it has ever been before: through Jesus Christ our
Lord. Amen.

*The Reading Lesson:* Proverbs 8.12-21

*Prayer*

O God, we need your forgiveness.

> For the failure to do what we know is right;
>
> For the failure to love and to forgive and to serve
> others as we know we ought to do;
>
> For the failure to be what we can be and to do what we
> can do:
>
> > Forgive us, O God.

O God, we need your help,

> Help not so much to know what is right—we know that
> already—but help to do what is right;
>
> Help to resist the temptations which come to us from
> inside ourselves and from the invitations and the
> persuasions of others;
>
> Help not to be afraid to do the right thing;
>
> Help to be what we can be and to do what we can do:
>
> > Give us this help, O God.

O God, we owe you thanks.

> Thanks for our health and our strength;
> Thanks for all the things we enjoy and for all the people who are dear to us;
> Thanks for giving us life and for giving us everything that makes life so gloriously worthwhile;
> Thanks for Jesus our Saviour and Friend:

Send us out from this place to show our gratitude by the faithfulness of our lives.

## *A Prayer of Dean Vaughan*

O Lord God, give us grace to set a good example to all amongst whom we live, to be just and true in all our dealings, to be strict and conscientious in the discharge of every duty, pure and temperate in all enjoyment, kind and charitable and courteous towards all men; that so the mind of Jesus Christ may be formed in us, and all men may take knowledge of us that we are his disciples: through Jesus Christ our Lord. Amen.

## *The Blessing*

The love of God, the grace of our Lord Jesus Christ, the fellowship of the Holy Spirit be with us all. Amen.

# GRATITUDE AND PENITENCE

*The Opening Prayer*

O God, our Father, grant that this short time of worship may not be to us a nuisance and something with which we really cannot be bothered. Grant that it may not be a mere formality which has to be pushed through because it is the custom. Give us tonight hearts which really want to tell you of their gratitude for your gifts and of their sorrow for their mistakes. And make us to come with gladness, to wait with expectation, and to worship with concentration this night: through Jesus Christ our Lord. Amen.

*The Reading Lesson:* Isaiah 55.1-11

*Prayer*

O God, our Father, we bring you thanks this night for all the gifts which you have given to us.

We thank you

> That you have made us alive;
> That you have given us this fair world to live in;
> That you have given us healthy bodies and sane minds;
> That you have given us work to do and leisure to enjoy;
> That you have surrounded us with friends to delight in and dear ones to love;
> That you have given us Jesus as our Master, our Saviour, and our Lord.

O God, our Father, we bring you this night our sorrow for all the wrong things we have done.

Forgive us,

> For our failure to work as we ought to work, and to study as we ought to study;

144

For our failure to forgive as we ought to forgive, and
    to be kind as we ought to be kind;
For the failure to be true to our friends, to be loyal to
    our loved ones, to be faithful and obedient to you;
For our failure to do what we know we ought to do,
    and to be what we know we ought to be.

Help us in the days to come to show the reality of our
gratitude by living more nearly as we ought.

*A Prayer of George Matheson*

O Divine Spirit, who in all the events of life art knocking
at the door of my heart, help me to respond to thee. I would
not be driven blindly as the stars over their courses. I would
not be made to work out thy will unwillingly, to fulfil thy
law unintelligently, to obey thy mandates unsympathetically.
I would take the events of my life as good and perfect gifts
from thee; I would receive even the sorrows of life as dis-
guised gifts from thee. I would have my heart open at all
times to receive—at morning, noon, and night; in spring and
summer and winter. Whether thou comest to me in sunshine
or in rain, I would take thee into my heart joyfully. Thou
art thyself more than the sunshine; thou art thyself com-
pensation for the rain; it is thee, and not thy gifts, I crave;
knock and I shall open unto thee.   Amen.

*The Blessing*

The grace of the Lord Jesus Christ be with us all.   Amen.

# TO KEEP LIFE HAPPY

*The Opening Prayer*

Grant, O God, that here tonight in the light of your presence, and in comparison with Jesus, we may see our lives as they are and life as it ought to be. Give us true sorrow for our failure to be what we ought to be, and then give us the strength and the determination to be what you mean us to be : through Jesus Christ our Lord. Amen.

*The Reading Lesson:* Luke 20.19-26

*Prayer*

O God, keep us from the things which are bound to make life unhappy.

Keep us from

> The eyes which can always find some fault to see;
> The tongue which can always find something to grumble about;
> The heart which can always find some grudge and some bitterness to cherish.

Keep us from

> The perverseness which does not want anything it gets, and which always wants what it has not got;
> The ingratitude which does not even realize what it is getting;
> The attitude of mind which lives in continual resentment.

Give us

> The even temper which can take things as they come;
> The sense of humour which can always find some cause to smile;

> The gratitude which can always find something for
> which to be thankful;
> The cheerfulness which not all earth's shadows and dis-
> appointments can extinguish.

Give us the spirit which can enjoy life, and which can help others to enjoy it.

### A Prayer of D. L. Moody

Use me then, my Saviour, for whatever purpose, and in whatever way, thou mayest require. Here is my poor heart, an empty vessel; fill it with thy grace. Here is my sinful and troubled soul; quicken it and refresh it with thy love. Take my heart for thine abode; my mouth to spread abroad the glory of thy name; my love and all my powers for the advancement of thy believing people; and never suffer the steadfastness and confidence of my faith to waver—that so at all times I may be enabled from the heart to say, Jesus needs me, and I him. Amen.

### The Blessing

The Lord bless us and keep us. The Lord make his face shine upon us and be gracious unto us. The Lord lift up his countenance upon us and give us peace. Amen.

147

# THE IDEAL AND THE WAY TO IT

*The Opening Prayer*

Lord Jesus, you are the Way, the Truth and the Life. Help us tonight,

> To see more clearly the way we ought to take;
> To know more fully the truth we ought to know;
> To go out to live more faithfully the life we ought to live.

This we ask for your love's sake. Amen.

*The Reading Lesson:* Luke 11.1-13

*Prayer*

Eternal and ever-blessed God, equip us, not only to see, but also to attain, the ideal.

Grant unto us,

> The wisdom to know what is right, and the courage to do it;
> The clear sight to see the right way, and the perseverance to walk in it;
> The vision to see the ideal, and the discipline to toil towards it.

Help us never to be satisfied

> With words without deeds;
> With plans without performance;
> With schemes without results;
> With dreams without toil to make the dream come true.

Teach us

> That the way to the stars is always steep;
> That sweat is the price of all things precious;
> That there never can be any crown without a cross.

148

So make us willingly to spend life that we may gain life, and to take up our cross and follow in the footsteps of our Lord and Master, Jesus Christ.

## A Prayer of Benjamin Jenks

O Lord, renew our spirits and draw our hearts unto thyself, that our work may not be to us a burden, but a delight; and give us such a mighty love to thee as may sweeten all our obedience. O, let us not serve thee with the spirit of bondage as slaves, but with the cheerfulness and gladness of children, delighting ourselves in thee and rejoicing in thy work. Amen.

## The Blessing

The grace of our Lord Jesus Christ, the love of God, and the fellowship of the Holy Spirit be upon us all this night and stay with each one of us always. Amen.

# FAILURE, SUCCESS, ROUTINE

*The Opening Prayer*

O God, our Father, tonight we come to you,
>To hear your word as the Bible is read;
>To sing your praise in the poetry and the music of
>our hymns;
>To speak to you in our prayers;
>To listen to you in our silence.

Help us tonight to worship you in spirit and in truth:
through Jesus Christ our Lord.   Amen.

*The Reading Lesson:* John 15.1-14

*Prayer*

O God, our Father, we ask you tonight specially to bless
those who feel that they have failed:

>Those who have fallen to temptation,
>>and who regret it;
>Those who have hurt their loved ones,
>>and who are ashamed of it;
>Those who have failed in some task,
>>and who know that it is their own fault.

We ask you tonight specially to bless those who have suc-
ceeded:

>Those who have done well,
>>that they may be kept from pride;
>Those who are happy and carefree,
>>that they may never feel that they can do without
>>you;
>Those who feel that there is nothing to worry about,
>>that over-confidence may not bring them disaster.

We ask you to bless those for whom life is very ordinary:
> Those who feel that nothing ever happens;
> Those who feel that life is dull and uninteresting;
> Those who are bored and fed up with the routine of everyday.
>> Teach all such that it is in the common tasks they find or miss their destiny and their reward.

You know us better than we know ourselves. Bless us, not as we ask, but as you in your wisdom know that we need.

## A Prayer of J. H. Jowett

O God, keep me sensitive to the grace that is round about me. May the familiar not become neglected! May I see thy goodness in my daily bread, and may the comfort of my home take my thoughts to the mercy seat of God! Amen.

## The Blessing

May grace, mercy and peace from Father, Son and Holy Spirit, one God, rest on and abide with each one of us now and for evermore. Amen.

# THE USE OF LIFE

*The Opening Prayer*

We come to you tonight, O God, because we need you.
    We cannot work well by day without your help, and we
        cannot sleep well at night without your blessing.
We come to you tonight, O God, because we love you.
    We want to speak to you and we want to listen to you
        speaking to us before the day ends and the night comes.
So come to meet us as we have come to meet you: through
Jesus Christ our Lord.   Amen.

*The Reading Lesson:* Colossians 3.16—4.6

*Prayer*

O God, help us to think of life as we ought to think of it,
and to use life as it ought to be used.

Help us always to remember,
        That you gave us life,
            and that it is not ours to do with as we like;
        That life comes to an end,
            and that we must not waste it when we have it;
        That we cannot tell what a day will bring to us,
            and so we must not put things off until tomorrow
            in case tomorrow never comes.
Help us,
        To use life wisely and not foolishly;
        To use life generously and not selfishly;
        To use life strenuously and not lazily;
        To use life with discipline and not with self-indulgence;
        To use life in the constant memory that one day we
            shall give account of it to you.

To that end help us always to walk with Jesus who is the Lord of all good life and who came to give us life and life more abundantly.

## A Prayer of Thomas à Kempis

O Lord, thou knowest what is best for us, let this or that be done as thou shalt please. Give what thou wilt, and how much thou wilt, and when thou wilt. Deal with me as thou thinkest good, and as best pleaseth thee. Set me where thou wilt and deal with me in all things as thou wilt. Behold, I am thy servant, prepared for all things; for I desire not to live unto myself, but unto thee; and O that I could do it worthily and perfectly!   Amen.

## The Blessing

The blessing of God, Father, Son and Holy Spirit, be with us all now and stay with each one of us always.   Amen.

# GREAT THINGS GONE WRONG

*The Opening Prayer*

O God, the Father,

> make us sure this night of the power which has
> created us, and of the love which always sustains us.

O Jesus Christ, the Son,

> make us sure this night of the love which died for
> us and of the risen presence which is with us now,
> always and to the end of the world.

O Holy Spirit, the Helper,

> make us sure this night that you will teach us what
> we ought to say, what we ought to do, where we
> ought to go, if we ask your help in faith and accept
> it in obedience.

And to Father, Son, and Holy Spirit be all the honour and
all the glory, world without end.   Amen.

*The Reading Lesson:* Psalm 121

*Prayer*

O God, tonight we specially ask you to help us never to
allow the great things of life to go wrong.

Help us never to allow

> Caution to become cowardice,
>
> or courage to become recklessness.

Help us never to allow

> Carefulness to become meanness,
>
> or spending to become squandering.

Help us never to allow

> Honesty to become discourtesy,
>
> or politeness to become evasion of the truth.

154

Help us never to allow
> Liberty to become licence,
> or pleasure to become sin.

Help us never selfishly to make use of our friends, never thoughtlessly to take our loved ones for granted, never to make your love an excuse for thinking that we can do what we like. Help us always to remember how we have been loved and to try to be more worthy of it.

### A Prayer for the Tongue

Set a watch upon our tongue, O Lord, that we may never speak the cruel word which is untrue; or, being true, is not the whole truth; or, being wholly true, is merciless; for the love of Jesus Christ our Lord.   Amen.

### The Blessing

The Lord preserve our going out and our coming in from this time forth for evermore.   Amen.

# BODY, MIND AND SPIRIT

*The Opening Prayer*

> O be with us, gracious Father,
>> While before thy feet we bow;
> Let the angel of thy presence
>> Hover o'er thy temple now.

Hear this our prayer, through Jesus Christ our Lord. Amen.

*The Reading Lesson:* Romans 12.1, 2, 9-21

*Prayer*

O God, our Father, you have made us body, mind and spirit. Help us to make each part of ourselves what it ought to be.

You have given us bodies.

Help us to keep them in health. Grant that we may never find pleasure in any habit or indulgence which would injure our bodies. Help us to keep them fit, and make us willing to accept the discipline which will keep them from becoming flabby and unhealthy.

You have given us minds.

Help us to study to fit ourselves for the trade, the craft, the profession by which one day we will make a living for ourselves and for those we love. Keep us from the lazy mind which will not learn, and from the shut mind that cannot learn. Help us every day to enrich our minds by adding some new thing to our store of knowledge.

You have given us spirits.

Help us to remember that there is a bit of us which will always go on, that there is a part of us which can speak to you, and to which you can speak. Help us to remember that we are creatures of eternity as well as of time; and so in this world help us to fit ourselves for the life into which we will one day enter.

## A Prayer for the Compassion of Christ

O Lord Jesus, who wast moved with compassion for all who had gone astray, with indignation for all who suffered wrong: inflame our hearts with the burning fire of thy love, that with thee we may seek out the lost, with thee have mercy on the fallen, and with thee stand fast for truth and righteousness, both now and always. Amen. (E. Milner-White and G. W. Briggs.)

## The Blessing

The blessing of God the Father, the Son and the Holy Spirit, be on us all now and stay with each one of us always. Amen.

# THE CLEANSING OF SELFISHNESS

*The Opening Prayer*

O God, our Father, make us for this time of worship very conscious and very aware of your presence.

Help us to remember your holiness, that there may be reverence in our hearts.

Help us to remember your love that we may be quite sure that you are the Father who is ready to welcome all who come to him: through Jesus Christ our Lord. Amen.

*The Reading Lesson:* Psalm 95.1-6

*Prayer*

O Lord Jesus, you have taught us that, if we wish to follow you, we must leave self behind. Keep us from all selfishness in our lives.

Keep us from being selfish in our aims and our ambitions,
   and help us to seek always to serve and never to rule.
Keep us from being selfish in the use of the gifts and the possessions which you have given to us,
   and help us always to give and to share, and never to keep and to hold.
Keep us from being selfish in our pleasures,
   and help us never to find pleasure in anything which would hurt another.
Keep us from being selfish in our treatment of other people, from being careless of their feelings, unsympathetic to their troubles, regardless of their convenience, from making use of them to suit ourselves.
   and help us always to think of others as much as we think of ourselves.

Help us to find our pleasure in helping others, our happiness in making others happy, our joy in, like our Master, going about doing good.

## An unknown Saint's Evening Prayer

O God, who hast drawn over the weary day the restful veil of night, enfold us in thy heavenly peace. Lift from our hands our tasks, and all through the night bear in thy bosom the full weight of our burdens and sorrows, that in untroubled slumber we may press our weariness close to thy strength, and win new power for the morrow's duties from thee who givest to thy beloved in sleep: through Jesus Christ our Lord. Amen.

## The Blessing

Now unto him that is able to do exceedingly abundantly above all that we ask or think, be glory in the Church throughout all ages world without end; and may the blessing of God, Father, Son and Holy Spirit be on us all now and stay with each one of us this night and always. Amen.

*The Opening Prayer*

> Grant us thy truth to make us free,
>    And kindling hearts to burn for thee;
> Till all thy holy altars claim,
>    One heavenly light, one holy flame.

O God, our Father, give us this night the light of thy truth in our minds and the fire of thy love in our hearts: through Jesus Christ our Lord. Amen.

*The Reading Lesson:* Micah 6.6-8

*Prayer*

O God, you have given us life. Help us to live in such a way that we shall make the contribution to life which we ought to make.

Keep us from living ungratefully,
   And help us always to remember all that has been done for us and all that we have received.
Keep us from living irresponsibly,
   And help us always to remember that we shall one day answer to you for the way in which we have used everything which you have given to us.
Keep us from living carelessly,
   And grant that we may never bring shame to ourselves or hurt and sorrow to others because we did not stop to think.
Keep us from living selfishly,
   And grant that our comfort, our pleasure, our wishes, our aims, our ambitions may not be the only things which matter to us. Help us to remember that we have

received our time, our talents and our money to use not only for ourselves, but also for our fellowmen.

Keep us from living dangerously,

And grant that we may never foolishly flirt with temptation or play with fire. Help us to have nothing to do with the things and the pleasures which we know are wrong.

Keep us from living unsocially,

And help us to take our full part in the life and the work and the service of the community.

Keep us from living exclusively,

And grant that we may never shut any man out from our society because of his colour, his party, or his creed.

## A Homegoing Prayer

Grant us thy peace upon our homeward way;
With thee began, with thee shall end the day.
Guard thou the lips from sin, the hearts from shame,
Which in this house have called upon thy name.

## The Blessing

The blessing of God, Father, Son and Holy Spirit, be on us and remain with us all.   Amen.

# OUR CHURCH, OUR COUNTRY, AND OUR WORLD

*The Opening Prayer*

> Jesus, stand among us
> In thy risen power;
> Let this time of worship
> Be a hallowed hour.

Lord Jesus, help us this night indeed to feel that you are here. This we ask for your love's sake.   Amen.

*The Reading Lesson:* I Timothy 2.1-7

*Prayer*

Tonight in our prayers let us send our thoughts out beyond ourselves and beyond our fellowship into the wider world.

*First of all, let us pray for the Church*

> O God, our Father, bless your Church. What in her is dark, illumine; what is low, raise and support; what is wanting, supply; what is in error, take away. Make her here and all over the world a real fellowship in which there are no quarrels and no divisions, no distinctions of race or colour, of class or party, a fellowship in which all are really one. And help us in our church to work and to pray to make the Church like that.

*Now let us pray for our country*

> O God, our Father, help us to love our country with a passion so strong and so true that we shall be jealous for its honour and instant in its service, and that we shall not rest until we have made this a land where men

walk in the freedom of the truth and in the light of knowledge. To that end help us to find leaders whose only master is their conscience and who ever speak with you before they speak to their fellow men.

## Now let us pray for the whole world

O God, who made of one blood all nations who dwell in the world, bless this world. Bring quickly the day when colour and race shall no longer divide men. Give your help in those places where new nations are being born, and grant that bitterness and hatred may not destroy brotherhood and peace. And hasten the time when the knowledge of yourself will cover the earth as the waters cover the sea and when men shall no longer even speak of war.

## A Prayer of Saint Bernard

O Jesus, ever with us stay,
    Make all our moments calm and bright;
Chase the dark night of sin away,
    Shed o'er the world thine own true light.

## The Blessing

The grace of the Lord Jesus Christ be with us all.   Amen.

# THE PEACE OF GOD

*The Opening Prayer*

The Psalmist thanked God that God had kept his feet from falling, his eyes from tears, and his soul from death. Let us ask God to do that for us.

Eternal and ever-blessed God, grant us,

> The light and the guidance which keep our feet from falling;
>
> The comfort and the consolation which will keep our eyes from tears;
>
> The life eternal which will keep our souls from death: through Jesus Christ our Lord. Amen.

*The Reading Lesson:* Isaiah 11.1-9

*A Prayer for Peace*

O God, you are the God of peace; help us to find peace.

Help us to have peace in our own homes, and save us from the irritability, the selfishness, the bad temper which make us so difficult to live with.

Help us to have peace at our work. Take away the suspicion and distrust between employer and employee, between master and man; and help all to find a way to live in a partnership for the common good.

Help us to have peace within the Church. Help us to get rid of the divisions between the different branches of the Church; and within our own congregations help us never to let anything disturb the friendship and the fellowship which should be there.

Help us to find peace between race and race. Help us never to dislike a man and never to look down upon him because of his race or colour. Help us to see in every man a brother for whom Christ died.

Help us to find peace between nation and nation. Help men to see the folly of war and to realize that no nation can ever really win any war. Give to this and to every other country leaders who seek for peace, and help us not to rest until we have built up a civilization in which men shall never even speak of war.

### King Charles the First's Prayer

O Lord, make the way plain before me. Let thy glory be my end, thy Word my rule; and then, thy will be done. Amen.

### The Blessing

The grace of the Lord Jesus Christ be with us all.  Amen.

*The Opening Prayer*

Grant us, this night, O God, clear sight to see the way we ought to take, and courage and perseverance to follow it to the end. Give us humility to ask what is your will for us, and give us trust and obedience to say, Your will be done: through Jesus Christ our Lord. Amen.

*The Reading Lesson:* Psalm 96

*Prayer*

Help us, O God, to fulfil all the duties which life brings to us.

Help us,

> To honour our parents;
> To be loyal to our friends;
> To be true to our loved ones.

Help us,

> To be diligent in our studies;
> To be conscientious in our work;
> To be wise in our pleasure.

Help us,

> To be brave in danger;
> To be strong in temptation;
> To be uncomplaining in pain;
> To be cheerful in disappointment.

Help us,

> To remain humble in prosperity;
> To remain hopeful in adversity.

And help us at all times so to live that our life and conduct may make it plain that we belong to you.

## A Prayer of Rabindranath Tagore

Give us the strength lightly to bear our joys and sorrows.

Give us the strength to make our love fruitful in service.

Give us the strength never to disown the poor, or bend our knees before insolent might.

Give us the strength to raise our minds high above daily trifles.

And give us the strength to surrender our strength to thy will with love.  Amen.

## The Blessing

May God, our heavenly Father, bless and keep us his children this night and for ever.  Amen.

# THE THINGS WE OWE

*The Opening Prayer*

Grant, O God, that this night each of us may find in you that which we need. Grant that

> The perplexed may find guidance;
> The tempted may find resistance power;
> The doubting may find certainty;
> The sad may find comfort;
> The lonely may find friendship.

Out of your all-sufficient grace supply our every need: through Jesus Christ our Lord. Amen.

*The Reading Lesson:* Psalm 8

*Prayer*

Help us, O God, to give to all with whom we come into contact that which we ought to give.

Help us to give to our parents, honour and obedience.

Help us to give to our teachers, respect and attention.

Help us to give to our employers, our best and most careful work.

Help us to give to friends and to those who love us, our unfailing loyalty.

Help us to give thanks to those who help us, and forgiveness to those who hurt us.

Help us to share the joy of those who are happy, and the sorrow of those who are sad.

Help us to help those whose work is hard, to praise those who have done well, and to sympathize with those who have failed.

## A Prayer of J. H. Jowett

Grant that we may walk as Christ walked; grant that what the Spirit was in him, such he may be also in us; grant that our lives may be refashioned after the pattern of his life; grant that we may do today here on earth what Christ would have done, and in the way he would have done it; grant that we may become vessels of his grace, instruments of his will, to thy glory and honour: through Jesus Christ our Lord. Amen.

## The Blessing

May God, the Fountain of all blessing, fill us with the understanding of sacred knowledge. May he keep us sound in faith, steadfast in hope, and persevering in patient charity. And may the blessing of the Father, the Son and the Holy Spirit, and the peace of the Lord be always with us. Amen.

# FAITHFUL IN EVERYTHING

*The Opening Prayer*

O God, our Father, tonight we have met for this short time
to read your book and to pray. Help us,

> To study your Book. that we may understand what it has
> to say to us;
>
> To obey your Book, that we may be saved from all errors
> and mistakes;
>
> To trust your Book, that we may be able to go on and to
> meet anything that life will bring to us in courage and
> in hope.

This we ask for your love's sake.   Amen.

*The Reading Lesson:* Isaiah 58.1-12

*Prayer*

O God, you are the Lord of all good life; help us to be faithful in everything which you have given us to do.

Help us to be conscientious and honest in our work, that
nothing we do may be less than our best.

Help us to be diligent and careful in our study, that we
may be able to understand, to remember and to use that
which we read and discover.

Help us to be regular in our daily reading of your word,
that no day may pass without your Book being in our
hands.

Help us to be faithful in our attendance both at church and
at this fellowship, that we may find joy in worshipping
and in talking with others who are trying to follow Jesus.

Help us never to forget each day to pray, that we may begin,
continue and end each day in thinking of you.

So help us to make of life what you meant it to be.

*Sir Thomas More's Prayer*

Give us, O Lord, an humble, quiet, peaceable, patient, tender, and charitable mind, and in all our thoughts, words, and deeds a taste of thy Holy Spirit. Give us, O Lord, a lively faith, a firm hope, a fervent charity, a love of thee. Take from us all lukewarmness in meditation, dullness in prayer. Give us fervour and delight in thinking of thee and thy grace, thy tender compassion towards us. The things that we pray for, good Lord, give us grace to labour for: through Jesus Christ our Lord. Amen.

*The Blessing*

May the Lord lead us when we go, and keep us when we sleep, and talk with us when we wake; and may the peace of God, which passeth all understanding, keep our hearts and minds in Christ Jesus our Lord. Amen.

## The Opening Prayer

Grant to us tonight, O God, the seeing eye, the hearing ear, the understanding mind and the loving heart, so that we may see your glory, and hear your word, and understand your truth, and answer to your love: through Jesus Christ our Lord. Amen.

## The Reading Lesson: I Corinthians 1.18-31

## Prayer

O God, touch every part of us with your Spirit and your power.

Be in our hearts, that every unclean and impure thought may be banished from them.

Be in our minds, that they may be eager to learn, adventurous to think, and retentive to remember.

Be in our eyes that they may never linger on any forbidden thing, or find delight in looking at that which is soiled.

Be in our ears that, above the many voices of the clamorous world, we may hear your still small voice speaking to us.

Be upon our hands, that we may do an honest day's work for ourselves and that we may ever help others.

Be upon our feet, that we may never stray from the way in which we ought to go.

So be on every part of us that we may be able to take all life and bring it as an offering to you.

## An Evening Prayer

Almighty God, our heavenly Father, abide with us as the

day draws to its close. Grant us the peace of pardoned children, and the security of those who are at home in thy house, fed at thy table, comforted at thy knee, and guarded by thine unsleeping watch: for thy Name's sake.   Amen.

*The Blessing*

The grace of our Lord Jesus Christ be with us all.   Amen.

# THE STRENGTH OF GOD

*The Opening Prayer*

Grant, O God, that we may never grudge any time that we give to you, but that we may always be,

> Eager to hear your word;
> Glad to sing your praise;
> Ready to hear your truth;
> Happy to pray to you.

This we ask through Jesus Christ our Lord.   Amen.

*The Reading Lesson:* Lamentations 3.22-27

*Prayer*

O God, Source of all strength and goodness,

Help us to resist the things which by ourselves we cannot resist,

> To overcome the temptations which fascinate us;
> To break the habits which enslave us;
> To say No to anything which invites us to set foot on the wrong way.

Help us to do and to be all the things which by ourselves we cannot do and be.

> We have never been as good as we could be;
> We have never done anything as well as it could be done;
> Life has never been what it might have been and could have been.

Give us the strength and wisdom to be what you meant us to be, and to do what you meant us to do, so that we may fulfil the purpose for which you sent us into this your world.

## A Prayer of Charles Kingsley

Guide us, teach us, and strengthen us, O Lord, we beseech
thee, until we become such as thou wouldst have us to be;
pure, gentle, truthful, high-minded, courteous, generous,
able, dutiful and useful: for thy honour and thy glory.
Amen.

## The Blessing

The love of God, the grace of our Lord Jesus Christ, the
fellowship of the Holy Spirit be upon us, and upon all whom
we love here and everywhere, and stay with each one of us
and them this night and always. Amen.

# FOR OBEDIENCE

*The Opening Prayer*

O God, our Father, grant that our meeting with you tonight may make us able to accept willingly all the disciplines which life brings to us:

> The discipline of work and study at school, at college, at university, at our trade or profession, that in our youth we may store our minds with that which we shall one day use for you and for our fellowmen;
>
> The discipline of witness that we may never be ashamed to show whose we are and whom we serve;
>
> The discipline of service, that in our home and in our church we may, like our Master, be among those who serve.

This we ask for Jesus' sake. Amen.

*The Reading Lesson:* John 15.9-17

*Prayer*

O God, help us, in our lives to have that obedience which alone can make life truly great. Help us to have,

> Obedience to our parents, always remembering that experience and the years have made them wise;
>
> Obedience to the laws we read in your book, that we may never be guilty of breaking any of your commandments;
>
> Obedience to conscience, knowing that it is your voice speaking inside us;

Obedience to the highest that we know, that we may
never do or be anything that is less than our best;
Obedience to our traditions, that we may never soil,
or tarnish, or let down the heritage into which we
have entered;
Obedience to Jesus, that we may be his friends, because we do what he commands us.

## Queen Elizabeth's Prayer

Create in me, O Lord, a new heart, and so renew my Spirit
that thy law may be my study, thy truth my delight, thy
Church my care, thy people my crown, thy righteousness
my pleasure, thy service my government; so shall this kingdom through thee be established with peace. Amen.

## The Blessing

The grace of the Lord Jesus Christ be with us all. Amen.

# GOD'S CLEANSING POWER

*The Opening Prayer*

O God, you have shown us the more excellent way; help us
always to walk in it.

> Restrain us when we are like to go astray;
> Refresh us when we are tired;
> Encourage us when we are depressed;
> Help us, when we fall, to rise and to begin again.

And so keep us in the way everlasting, until in your good
time we reach our journey's end: through Jesus Christ our
Lord.  Amen.


*The Reading Lesson:* Proverbs 15.13-21


*Prayer*

O God, our Father, Giver of all purity and grace, cleanse
and strengthen every part of us.

> Be on our lips that we may speak no false, no cruel,
>    no ugly, no impure word.
> Be in our eyes that we may look not for things to
>    criticize, but for things to praise, that our eyes
>    may never linger on any forbidden thing, but ever
>    look on the things which are beautiful and good.
> Be in our minds that they always be brave to think,
>    eager to learn, and retentive to remember, and that
>    all our thoughts may be pure.
> Be in our hearts, that we may always love that which
>    is highest and best, and that we may surrender
>    them in loyalty and in devotion to you.

## A Prayer of Lancelot Andrewes

May the power of the Father govern us. May the wisdom of the Son enlighten us. May the operation of the Holy Spirit quicken us. O God, we beseech thee, guard our souls; sustain our bodies; exalt our senses; direct our course; regulate our manners; bless our undertakings; fulfil our petitions; inspire us with holy thoughts; pardon what is past; rectify what is present; order what is to come; and all for the sake of Jesus Christ our Lord and Saviour, who alone can make us perfect as he is perfect.   Amen.

## The Blessing

May grace, mercy and peace from Father, Son and Holy Spirit, one God, rest on us all now and remain with each one of us always.   Amen.

*The Opening Prayer*

O God, our Father, grant that our meeting here together
with you tonight may make our lives

>> Useful in service;
>> Beautiful with love;
>> Strong in faith;

so that we may go out to serve you and to serve our fellowmen better than before: through Jesus Christ our Lord.
Amen.


*The Reading Lesson:* Ruth 1.1-18


*Prayer*

O God, you have made our hearts such that loyalty is the
most precious quality in this life. Help us to have this
loyalty.

> Help us to have loyalty to our principles, so that every-
> one may know where we stand and what we stand
> for.
> Help us to have loyalty to the truth, so that everyone
> may know that our word can be trusted absolutely.
> Help us to have loyalty to our friends, so that we will
> never let them down, and so that they can be certain
> that we will stand by them in any company and in
> any circumstances.
> Help us to be loyal to our loved ones and to be true to
> them through all the chances and the changes of this
> life.

Help us to be loyal to you, so that we will never be
ashamed to show whose we are and whom we serve,
and so that we shall be proud to let the world see
that for us Jesus Christ is Lord.

## *A Prayer of Clement of Rome*

We beseech thee, Lord and Master, to be our help and
succour. Save those who are in tribulation; have mercy on
the lonely; lift up the fallen; show thyself unto the needy;
heal the ungodly; convert the wanderers of thy people; feed
the hungry; raise up the weak; comfort the faint-hearted.
Let all the peoples know that thou art God alone, and Jesus
Christ is thy Son, and we are thy people and the sheep of
thy pasture: for the sake of Christ Jesus. Amen.

## *The Blessing*

The Lord bless us and keep us. The Spirit of the Lord
cleanse and purify our inmost hearts, and enable us to shun
all evil. The Lord enlighten our understandings and cause
the Light of his Truth to shine into our hearts. The Lord
fill us with faith and love towards him. The Lord be with
us day and night, in our coming in and going out, in our
sorrow and in our joy. And bring us at length into his
eternal rest. Amen.

*The Opening Prayer*

Help us, O God, now and at all times,
>To respect ourselves;
>To love our fellowmen;
>To reverence you;

that we may do nothing,
>To shame ourselves;
>To injure others;
>To grieve you:

through Jesus Christ our Lord.   Amen.


*The Reading Lesson:* Proverbs 3.1-12


*Prayer*

O God, save us from being unwise enough to refuse the discipline which we ought to accept.

>Keep us from being too proud to ask for advice.

>Keep us from being too self-conceited to accept guidance.

>Keep us from being too self-willed to endure rebuke.

>Keep us from foolishly disregarding the experience of those who are older and wiser than we are.

>Keep us from the self-confidence that cannot believe that it can be wrong, and which can see no point of view but its own.

Make us wise enough to realize our own ignorance, and to recognize our own weakness, that we may come to you who are the source of all wisdom and all strength.

### The Bedouin Camel-Drivers' Prayer at Sunset

O Lord, be gracious unto us! In all that we hear or see, in all that we say or do, be gracious unto us. I ask pardon of the Great God. I ask pardon at the sunset, when every sinner turns to him. Now and for ever I ask pardon of God. O Lord, cover us from our sins, guard our children, and protect our weaker friends.

### The Blessing

May the Lord Jesus Christ fill us with spiritual joy, may his Spirit make us strong and tranquil in the truths of his promises. And may the blessing of the Lord come on us abundantly. Amen.

# THAT WE MAY NOT SPOIL THINGS

*The Opening Prayer*

O God, our Father, help us to find here tonight the power which will inspire us to goodness and restrain us from sin. Help us to find forgiveness for all the wrong things that we have done in the past and strength and grace to do better in the future: through Jesus Christ our Lord. Amen.

*The Reading Lesson:* Matthew 6.1-5, 16-18

*Prayer*

O God, our Father, keep us from doing things in a way that takes all the value out of them.

Keep us from doing things unwillingly and with a grudge, in a way that makes it quite clear that the whole thing is a nuisance to us.

Keep us from doing things so badly and so inattentively that they have to be done all over again.

Keep us from doing things in such a hurry that they are only half done.

Keep us from doing things in order to show off how good and how kind and how clever we are.

Help us to do everything in such a way that we would be happy to know that you are watching us and glad to offer what we have done to you.

*A Prayer of Archbishop Laud for the Church*

Gracious Father, we humbly beseech thee for thy universal Church. Fill it with all truth, in all truth with all peace. Where it is corrupt, purge it; where it is in error, direct it; where it is superstitious, rectify it; where anything is amiss, reform it; where it is right, strengthen and confirm it; where it is in want, furnish it; where it is divided and rent asunder, make up the breaches thereof, O thou Holy One of Israel: for the sake of Jesus Christ our Lord and Saviour. Amen.

*A Blessing of Aedelwald, a Saxon Bishop of the Ninth Century*

May God the Father bless us; may Christ take care of us; the Holy Spirit enlighten us all the days of our life.

The Lord be our Defender and Keeper of body and soul, both now and for ever to the ages of ages. Amen.

# GRATITUDE FOR GOD'S WORLD

*The Opening Prayer*

Grant unto us, O God, tonight
    Clear sight to see our own faults;
    Humility to confess and to acknowledge them;
    Resolution to mend and to cure them.
Help us to come to you that you may forgive us for our faults and that you may give us strength and grace to overcome them: through Jesus Christ our Lord. Amen.

*The Reading Lesson:* Psalm 65.9-13

*Prayer*

O God, Creator and Sustainer of all things, we thank you for the world in which we live.

    For night and day;
    For dark and light;
    For summer and winter:
        We thank you.
    For the sun and the rain and the wind;
    For earth and sea and sky;
    For all the changing seasons of the year:
        We thank you.
    For all the flowers and fruits and crops of earth;
    For all the wealth which nature offers to man;
    For the beauty and the bounty of this world:
        We thank you.
    For all that brings nourishment to our bodies and delight to our eyes;
    For all that brings pleasure to our hearts;

For all the materials which earth gives to our hands on
   which to work:
     We thank you, O God.
Grant that everything we see in this world may turn our
thoughts to you, the Maker and Creator and Sustainer of
it all.

## A Prayer of Alcuin

O Eternal Goodness, deliver us from evil. O Eternal Power,
be thou our support. Eternal Wisdom, scatter the darkness
of our ignorance. Eternal Pity, have mercy upon us. Grant
unto us that with all our hearts and minds and strength we
may evermore seek thy face; and finally bring us in thine
infinite mercy to thy holy presence. So strengthen our weakness that following in the footsteps of thy Blessed Son, we
may obtain mercy and enter into thy promised joy: through
Jesus Christ our only Saviour and Redeemer.   Amen.

## The Blessing

The grace of the Lord Jesus Christ be with us all.   Amen.

# THE TRUE WISDOM

*The Opening Prayer*

Help us this night, O God, to find the wisdom which will tell us,

What to do and what not to do;
When to act and when to refrain from action;
When to speak and when to keep silent.

So grant that, guided by you, we may be saved from all wrong thoughts, from all words which we would wish unsaid and from all deeds we would wish undone: through Jesus Christ our Lord. Amen.

*The Reading Lesson:* James 3.6-18 (RSV)

*Prayer*

Grant unto us this night, O God, to find the wisdom which is from above.

Give us the wisdom which is pure, that we may never use our minds to think or plan an evil thing;

The wisdom which is peaceable that we may live in friendship with all and in bitterness with none;

The wisdom which is gentle, that we may ever be quicker to sympathize than to criticize, and to praise than to condemn;

The wisdom which is open to reason, that we may not be stubborn and self-willed, but willing to listen to and to obey the truth;

The wisdom which is full of mercy, that we may be as kind to others as we would wish them to be to us;

The wisdom which is full of good fruits, that our lives may be lovely with the beauty of holiness.

## A Prayer of Thomas Aquinas

Give us, O Lord, a steadfast heart, which no unworthy affection may drag downwards; give us an unconquered heart, which no tribulation can wear out; give us an upright heart, which no unworthy purpose may tempt aside. Bestow upon us also, O Lord, understanding to know thee, diligence to seek thee, wisdom to find thee, and a faithfulness that may finally embrace thee: through Jesus Christ our Lord. Amen.

## The Blessing

The peace of God which passeth all understanding keep our hearts and minds in the knowledge and love of God, and of his Son Jesus Christ our Lord, and the blessing of God Almighty, the Father, the Son and the Holy Spirit, be amongst us and remain with us always. Amen.

# FOR PATIENCE

*The Opening Prayer*

Eternal God, so purify our minds this night that we may think your thoughts after you. So cleanse our hearts that we may love only the things which you command. So touch our lips that we may speak only what you tell us. So strengthen our feet that we may not stumble in the right path. So make lovely our lives that men may see in us the reflection of the Master whose we are and whom we seek to serve: through Jesus Christ our Lord. Amen.

*The Reading Lesson:* Proverbs 4.1-13

*Prayer*

O God, give us the patience which we need so much.

Give us patience with people;
Patience with those who need and ask our help;
Patience with those who need our sympathy;
Patience with those who want us to listen while they talk to us.

Give us patience with our work;
Patience to work and study until we make ourselves good craftsmen;
Patience to accept the discipline of learning, of training, and of practice;
Patience to persevere with every task we do until we finish it.

Give us patience with life;
Patience to accept things, even when we do not see either the meaning or the reason for them;

Patience when hopes are very slow to come true;
Patience to take the long view of things and not to be
discouraged.

O God, you are the God of all eternity with all time to work in, help us to learn to wait in patience and in hope.

*A Prayer of J. H. Jowett*

Our Father, teach us not only to do thy will, but how to do it. Teach us the best way of doing the best thing, lest we spoil the end by unworthy means: for the sake of Christ Jesus our Lord. Amen.

*The Blessing*

The grace of the Lord Jesus Christ, the love of God, and the fellowship of the Holy Spirit be with us all now and stay with each one of us always. Amen.

# THE GREATEST OF THESE

*The Opening Prayer*

Give us now, O God, the reverent mind, that for these few minutes we may forget everything except that you are here. This we ask for your love's sake.   Amen.

*The Reading Lesson:* I Corinthians 13.4-7 in the R.S.V.

*Prayer*

Let us ask God to give us this love.

*Love is patient and kind.*

O God, help us to be patient with people even when they are foolish and silly and annoying; and help us always to be as kind to others as we would wish them to be to us.

*Love is not jealous or boastful.*

O God, help us never to grudge other people their possessions or their successes, but to be as glad as if they were our own; and keep us from all pride and from all conceit that we may never boast of what we are, or have, or have achieved.

*Love is not arrogant or rude.*

O God, make us at all times courteous, as those who always remember that they are living in the presence of the King; and no matter what we are, and no matter who or what the other person is, help us never to look on anyone with contempt.

*Love does not insist on its own way, is not irritable or resentful.*

O God, help us,

  Not to sulk when we do not get our own way;

  Not to be irritable and difficult to live with, but to take things and people as they come;

Not to resent criticism and rebuke, even when we
think that we do not deserve it.

*Love does not rejoice at wrong, but rejoices in the right.*

O God, help us never to find any pleasure in any wrong
thing, but to find happiness only in doing the right, and in
helping others to do it.

*Love bears all things, believes all things, hopes all things,*
*endures all things.*

O God, help us

To bear insults, injuries, slights and never to grow bitter;

Never to lose our faith in Jesus our Lord;

Never to despair, however dark and difficult and dis-
couraging life may be;

To stick it out to the end, and never to give in.

O God, you are love; help us to show your love to others
every day in life. This we ask for your love's sake.   Amen.

*The Lord's Prayer in Verse by George Wither, who lived*
*between 1588 and 1667*

> Our Father which in heaven art,
>     We sanctify thy name;
> Thy kingdom come, thy will be done,
>     In heaven and earth the same.
> Give us this day our daily bread,
>     And us forgive thou so,
> As we on them that us offend
>     Forgiveness do bestow.
> Into temptation lead us not,
>     And us from evil free,
> For thine the Kingdom, Power, and Praise
>     Is and shall ever be.

*The Blessing*

May the blessing of God Almighty, the Father, the Son, and
the Holy Spirit, rest upon us and upon all our work and
worship done in his name. May he give us light to guide us,
courage to support us, and love to unite us, now and evermore.   Amen.

# THE LAW OF GOD

*The Opening Prayer*

O God, help us tonight to be wise enough to ask for your guidance and to be humble enough to take it; to be willing to listen to your commandments, and then to be ready to obey them: through Jesus Christ our Lord. Amen.

*The Reading Lesson:* Exodus 20.1-17

*Prayer*

Let us think of God's commandments, and let us ask him to help us to obey each one of them.

*You shall have no other gods before me.*

O God, help us to give to you and to your obedience the first and the highest place in our lives.

*You shall not make yourself a graven image.*

O God, help us never to give any man-made thing the first place in our lives, and never to allow the desire for money, fame, power, success to take the place in our hearts and lives which you should have.

*You shall not take the name of the Lord your God in vain.*

O God, grant that we may never make a statement in your name which is not absolutely true, and grant that we may never make a promise or a pledge in your name and break it.

*Remember the Sabbath day to keep it holy.*

O God, help us to use your day to help us to live better on the other six days of the week.

*Honour your father and your mother.*

O God, help us to remember the debt of love and gratitude, of obedience and respect which we owe to our parents, and never to fail to discharge it.

*You shall not kill.*
Save us, O God, from the anger, the bitterness, the hatred, which would make us wish to hurt or injure any living creature.

*You shall not commit adultery.*
Keep us, O God, in purity of thought, and word, and action, that we may keep our bodies, and our minds, and our hearts chaste and clean.

*You shall not steal.*
Keep us, O God, from ever taking that which we have no right to take, and make us so honest that we will never stoop to dishonesty, however slight.

*You shall not bear false witness.*
Keep us, O God, from all lies and from all untrue words, and especially from repeating the stories and the rumours which would take someone's good name away.

*You shall not covet.*
Teach us, O God, to be content with what we have, and to serve you with gladness wherever life has placed us.

Help us, O God, to keep these your laws that one day we may receive your reward.


*Anselm's Prayer*

Grant, O Lord God, that we may cleave to thee without parting, worship thee without wearying, serve thee without failing, faithfully seek thee, happily find thee, for ever possess thee, the one only God, blessed world without end. Amen.


*The Blessing*
The grace of our Lord Jesus Christ go with us all. Amen.

*The Opening Prayer*

O God, our Father, as tonight we wait on you, grant to us
                    Certainty for our doubts;
                    Strength for our temptations;
                    Power for our tasks;
                    Forgiveness for our sins:
through Jesus Christ our Lord.   Amen.

*The Reading Lesson:* Matthew 5.1-12

*Prayer*

Let us think of the blessedness of which Jesus taught, and
let us ask him to make us able to enter into it.

*Blessed are the poor in spirit.*

> Help us, O God, to realize our own poverty and our
> own helplessness, and help us to come to you that you
> may make us rich in the things which really matter.

*Blessed are they that mourn.*

> Help us, O God, to be sorry for all the wrong things
> that we have done, and help us to show that our sorrow
> is real by not doing them again.

*Blessed are the meek.*

> Grant to us, O God, such perfect self-control that we
> may completely master ourselves, so that we may be
> fit and able to serve and to lead others.

*Blessed are they which do hunger and thirst after righteous-
ness.*

> Help us, O God, to long for goodness as much as a
> starving man longs for food, and as much as a man

dying of thirst longs for water, so that we may be ready to do anything and to give up anything to be what we ought to be.

*Blessed are the merciful.*

O God, our Father, help us at all times to be kind, and help us never either thoughtlessly or deliberately to hurt anyone else; and grant that no one may ever appeal to us for help and not receive it.

*Blessed are the pure in heart.*

O God, our Father, keep all our thoughts and all our desires clean and pure so that even our secret and inmost hearts may be fit for you to see, and so that we may see you.

*Blessed are the peacemakers.*

O God, our Father, grant that we may never at any time be the cause of trouble or of quarrels between other people; and help us all in this fellowship to be one united band of brothers in you.

*Blessed are those who are persecuted for righteousness' sake.*

O God, help us to be glad when being a Christian costs us something, because then we have a chance to show that we are not ashamed to let it be seen that we belong to Jesus.

Hear this our prayer and grant us this blessedness, through Jesus Christ our Lord.

## A Prayer from Compline

Save us, O Lord, waking, and guard us sleeping, that awake we may watch with Christ, and asleep we may rest in peace: through Jesus Christ our Lord.  Amen.

## The Blessing

The grace of our Lord Jesus Christ go with us all.  Amen.

# JESUS' PRAYER

*The Opening Prayer*

O God, our Father, send out your light and your truth upon us now,

    Your light that we may see where we ought to go;

    Your truth that we may know what we ought to do,

So that, being guided and taught by you we may make no mistakes: through Jesus Christ our Lord. Amen.

*The Reading Lesson:* Matthew 6.5-14

*Prayer*

Let us think of Jesus' prayer, and let us make it really ours.

*Our Father which art in heaven.*

O God, you have taught us to call you Father. Help us to come to you just as easily and just as confidently as we come to our closest friend, sure that you are always ready and willing and able to help.

*Hallowed be thy name.*

O God, give us the gift of reverence, so that we may remember that, no matter where we are, you see our actions and you hear our words, so that we may with your help make life fit for you to see.

*Thy Kingdom come.*

O God, help us to do all we can to bring the time when all men will take you as their king, and help us to bring that time nearer by making you king in our own hearts.

*Thy will be done in earth as it is in heaven.*

O God, whatever happens to us when we try to walk your way, help us to say, Your will be done; and help us to remember that you will never ask us to do anything or to suffer anything except in love.

*Forgive us our debts as we forgive our debtors.*

O God, help us to forgive others, as we hope ourselves to be forgiven; and help us to remember that we cannot be forgiven, unless we are willing to forgive.

*Give us this day our daily bread.*

O God, our Father, give us strength and ability to work faithfully and well, so that we may gain the things we need for life. And help us to be grateful for all that we receive and always to share it with others.

*Lead us not into temptation, but deliver us from evil.*

O God, give us power to resist all our temptations and always to do the right, and, when things are difficult, help us to remember that we will never be tried beyond what we can bear, and that we will never be asked to do what we cannot with your help do.

*Erasmus' Prayer*

O Lord, Jesus Christ, who art the Way, the Truth, and the Life, we pray thee suffer us not to stray from thee, who art the Way, nor to distrust thee, who art the Truth, nor to rest in any other thing than thee, who art the Life. Teach us by thy Holy Spirit, what to believe, what to do, and wherein to take our rest. Amen.

*The Ascription of Thomas Ken and the Blessing*

> To God the Father, who first loved us, and made us accepted in the Beloved:
> To God the Son, who loved us, and washed us from our sins in his own blood:
> To God the Holy Spirit, who sheds the love of God abroad within our hearts:
>> Be all love and all glory
>>> For time and for eternity.

And may the blessing of God, Father, Son and Holy Spirit be on us all. Amen.

### The Opening Prayer

Lord Jesus, on this Easter Sunday evening, although we cannot see you, help us to feel that you are very near and close to us. Help us this Easter time to discover for ourselves that you are not a figure in a book, but that you are a living presence, nearer to us than breathing and closer than hands or feet. Help us tonight to know you as our risen, ever-living, ever-present Lord. This we ask for your love's sake. Amen.

### The Reading Lesson: John 20.1-18

### Prayer

O God, our Father, we thank you this Easter evening for every part of the life of Jesus.

We thank you for his life:

That he had to grow up and to learn just as we have to do;

That he had to go to school, and to learn a trade, and to work at a job, just as we have to do;

That he had to do a day's work, to earn a pay, to support a family, just as we have to do;

That he knows well what everyday work and life are like:
   We thank you, O God.

For his words of wisdom and his deeds of love;

For his kindness to the sick and the suffering and the sad;

For his friendship with all kinds of people, even with people with whom the respectable would have nothing to do:
   We thank you, O God.

200

We thank you for his death:
    For the courage which made him go to the Cross;
    For the obedience which made him accept your will without question;
    For the love which suffered and bore all that for us:
        We thank you, O God.

We thank you for his resurrection this Easter Day:
    That he conquered death and rose from the grave;
    That he is alive for ever more;
    That he is with us always even to the end of the world;
    That nothing in life or in death can separate us from him:
        We thank you, O God.

## An Easter Prayer of Gregory the Great

O God, who for our redemption didst give thine only-begotten Son to the death of the Cross, and by his glorious resurrection hast delivered us from the power of the enemy, grant us to die daily to sin that we may ever more live with him in the joy of his Resurrection: through Jesus Christ our Lord. Amen.

## The Blessing

May the blessing of God Almighty, the Father, the Son, and the Holy Spirit, rest upon us, and upon all our work and worship done in his name. May he give us Light to guide us, Courage to support us, and Love to unite us, now and ever more. Amen.

*The Opening Prayer*

O God, giver of all good gifts, at this time of the giving
and the receiving of gifts, help us to remember that Jesus
said: It is more blessed to give than to receive. And put
into our hearts that love which knows that true happiness
comes from making others happy, and true wealth from
sharing all we have: through Jesus Christ our Lord. Amen.

*The Reading Lesson:* John 1.1-14

*Prayer*

Lord Jesus, we remember that you were born into this
world on the first Christmas Day.

Help us to remember,
> that you were born in a stable and cradled in a manger,
>> and so keep us from coveting a wealth and a comfort,
>> an ease and a luxury which you never enjoyed.

Help us to remember,
> that there was no room for you in the inn,
>> and grant that our lives may never become so crowded
>> that there is no room in them for you.

Help us to remember,
> that to you there came the Shepherds and the Wise Men,
>> and grant that learned and simple, high and humble,
>> great and small may be joined together in worshipping
>> and in loving you.

Help us to remember,
> that you grew up in an ordinary home, and went to
> school, and worked in a carpenter's shop,

and so grant that we may think no task too humble
and too common for our hands to touch, when you,
the Lord of Glory, lived amidst the common things.

Help us to remember,
that you were obedient to your parents, and that you
grew in wisdom and in stature, and in favour with God
and man,
and so help us to honour our father and mother, to
discipline our bodies, and to live in such a way that
we will gain the respect of our fellowmen, and gladden
the heart of our father in heaven.

This we ask this Christmas Sunday for your love's sake.

*A Christmas Prayer from Memorials upon Several Occasions*

Lord God Almighty, Father of every family, against whom
no door can be shut: Enter into the homes of our land,
we beseech thee, with the angel of thy presence, to hallow
them in pureness and beauty of love; and by thy dear Son,
born in a stable, move our hearts to hear the cry of the
homeless, and to convert all sordid and bitter dwellings
into households of thine: through Jesus Christ our Lord.
Amen.

*The Blessing*

The grace of the Lord Jesus Christ be with us all.

# THE LAST SUNDAY OF THE YEAR

*The Opening Prayer*

On this last Sunday of the year, give us, O God,
   Gratitude for all the days that are past;
   Courage to meet the present;
   Hope that the best of life is still to come:
through Jesus Christ our Lord. Amen.

*The Reading Lesson:* Psalm 90.1-4, 12, 16, 17

*Prayer*

O God, our Father, as this year comes to an end we re-member all its days.

   Every happy hour and every happy day;
   Every new thing we have learned and seen and done;
   Every new friend we have made, and the old friends to
      whom we are closer than ever we were:
         We remember and give thanks with joy.

   Everything which was difficult to face or hard to bear,
      but out of which we came wiser in mind and
      stronger in character;
   Every failure and disappointment that has kept us
      humble;
   Everything that has·shown us how dangerous life can
      be, and how much we need you:
         We remember and give thanks with joy.

   Every task in which we failed;
   Every temptation to which we fell;
   Every person we hurt and failed and disappointed;
   Every word and deed for which we are sorry now:
         We remember and confess with sorrow.

All those for whom this has been a thrilling, an ex-
citing and a successful year,
that they may remember to give you thanks;
All those for whom this has been a sad year, and who
come to the end of it lonelier than they were,
that they may find comfort and courage to go on;
All those for whom this has been an ordinary year,
when nothing special seemed to happen,
that they may know that it is in life's routine they
win or lose their destiny:
Bless them all.

And help us now, made wise by the lessons life has taught
us, to go on to higher heights and nobler things.

*The Prayer on Winifred Holtby's Grave*

Give me work
Till my life shall end
And life
Till my work is done.

*The Blessing*
The grace of the Lord Jesus Christ go with us all.

*The Opening Prayer*

O God, the years make no difference to you, and you have given us the privilege of another year. As we pray to you tonight,

> Tell us what you want us to do with this year,
> And give us strength and courage and determination to do it:

through Jesus Christ our Lord. Amen.

*The Reading Lesson:* Philippians 2.1-14

*Prayer*

O God, our Father, help us not to live a life which is never any further on. Help us to learn from experience and not to make the same mistakes over and over again. Help us not to go on allowing the same temptations to conquer us, and the same faults to spoil life for ourselves and for others. Help us always to look upwards and always to move onwards, that each year our life may become more nearly what you wish it to be.

Throughout this year that lies ahead, give us,
> Diligence in learning,
>> that more and more we may store our minds with the knowledge that we can use for our fellow men and for you;
> Discipline in living,
>> that each day our character may become stronger and more reliable;

Strength of mind in deciding,
> that, when we have chosen the right course, nothing may deflect us from it, and that we may always be able to refuse any invitation to take any other way;

Loyalty in friendship,
> that we may never fail, or be untrue to, those who trust us.

Fidelity in love,
> that we may never bring sorrow or heartbreak to those who love us.

Grant that all through this year we may live in the presence and walk in the footsteps of Jesus our Lord.

*The New Year Prayer from the Order of Divine Service for Public Worship*

Eternal God, who makest all things new, and abidest for ever the same: Grant us to begin this year in thy faith, and to continue it in thy favour; that guided in all our doings, and guarded in all our days, we may spend our lives in thy service, and finally, by thy grace, attain the glory of everlasting life: through Jesus Christ our Lord. Amen.

*The Blessing*

The love of God, the grace of the Lord Jesus Christ, the fellowship of his Holy Spirit be with us all now and stay with each one of us through all this year and for ever. Amen.

This is Whitsuntide, and on this Sunday we remember how at Pentecost the Holy Spirit came
upon the disciples of Jesus. Let us ask God for
his Spirit now.

## The Opening Prayer

O God, our Father, help us tonight to experience what the
Holy Spirit can do for us. Grant that tonight your Spirit
may come into us, to enlighten our minds, to purify our
hearts, to strengthen our lives; and so grant that by the
help of your Spirit we may do, and be, and become, what
is impossible for us by ourselves: through Jesus Christ our
Lord. Amen.

*The Reading Lesson:* Acts 2.1-4, 12-21

*Prayer*

Let us think of what Jesus said that his Spirit would
do (John 14.17, 26; 15.13, 14).

Jesus called his Spirit, The Spirit of Truth.

O Lord Jesus, grant us through your Spirit to come to
know the truth, so that we may never have any doubt
about what we ought to believe and what we ought
to do.

Jesus said of the Spirit: He will teach you all things.

O Lord Jesus, give us the teachable mind and heart,
so that when your Spirit speaks to us we may listen
and learn and obey.

Jesus said of the Spirit: He will bring to your remembrance all that I have said to you.

O Lord Jesus, grant that your Spirit may come and compel us to remember you when we are likely to forget you, and grant that your Spirit may remind us of your commandments when we are tempted to break them.

Jesus said of the Spirit: He will guide you into all truth.

O Lord Jesus, help us to see that every great discovery and every great achievement, all beauty and all truth, in literature, art, drama, music, medicine, science, thought, is the work of your Spirit, using men even when they do not know that they are being used.

Jesus said of the Spirit: He will take what is mine and declare it unto you.

O Lord Jesus, when we do not really understand what we ought to do, and when we do not really understand the meaning for us of some of the things you said, grant that your Spirit may explain them to us, and make us wise enough to listen that we may know.

*A Prayer of the Spirit from* Daily Prayer *by Eric Milner-White and G. W. Briggs*

> O Holy Spirit,
> Giver of light and life,
> Impart to us thoughts higher than our own thoughts,
> and prayers better than our own prayers,
> and powers beyond our own powers,
> that we may spend and be spent
> in the ways of love and goodness,
> after the perfect image,
> of our Lord and Saviour Jesus Christ.
> Amen.

*The Blessing*

The blessing of God Almighty, Father, Son and Holy Spirit be on us now and never leave us. Amen.

# REMEMBRANCE DAY

*The Opening Prayer*

O God, our Father, we know that we have entered into a great heritage and a great tradition. We know that we owe our liberty and our freedom to men who throughout the years lived and suffered, and sacrificed and died, for truth and right. Help us this night to remember them with gratitude and to resolve to be worthy of them: through Jesus Christ our Lord. Amen.

*The Reading Lesson:* Hebrews 11.32—12.2

*Prayer*

O God, our Father, on this Sunday of Remembrance we remember all those to whom we owe the life and the privileges we possess, and we thank you for them.

For those who lived and suffered and died to give us,
> The freedom and good government we possess;
> The liberty of conscience and of speech, of thought
> and of worship which we enjoy;
>> We thank you.

For those who lived and suffered and died to find for us,
> New continents and new lands and new countries in
> the distant places of the earth;
> New ways to heal the disease and to ease the pain of
> the world;
>> We thank you.

For all who died in war, on land, at sea, and in the air;
For those who were wounded in body and mind so that
life could never be the same again;

For those who in every age and generation have laid
down their lives for their friends;
>>>>>>>>>>>>>>>>We thank you.

Above all for Jesus, the Captain of every heroic soul;
That he loved us and gave himself for us;
That for us he bore the Cross with all its pain and
shame;
>>>>>>>>>>>>>>>>We thank you.

Help us to remember this night all that this our life has
cost, and help us to resolve never to waste it and never to
soil it.

*A Prayer used by Cardinal Newman*

O Lord, support us all the day long of this troublous life,
until the shadows lengthen and the evening comes, and the
busy world is hushed, and the fever of life is over and our
work is done. Then, Lord, in thy mercy, grant us a safe
lodging, a holy rest, and peace at the last: through Jesus
Christ our Lord.   Amen.

*The Blessing*

Now may grace, and mercy, and peace from Father, Son
and Holy Spirit, one God, rest upon us all and remain with
each one of us always.   Amen.

# TO BE SAVED FROM THE FAULTS THAT SPOIL THE BEST

*The Invitation:* These words are sometimes found on the doors of old churches.

> Enter this door
> As if the floor
> Within were gold,
> And every wall
> Of jewels all
> Of wealth untold;
> As if a choir
> In robes of fire
> Were singing here.
> Nor shout, nor rush,
> But hush . . .
> For God is here.

Even so let us come to worship God tonight.

*The Reading Lesson:* II Corinthians 4

*Prayer*

O God, our Father, keep us from spoiling good things.

Make us wise,
   But save us from being conceited.
Make us clear-sighted,
   But save us from being unkind.
Make us honest,
   But save us from tactless or heartless discourtesy.
Make us efficient,
   But save us from being inhuman and unsympathetic.

Make us strong-willed,
    But save us from being stubborn.
Make us to enjoy life,
    But save us from making pleasure our only object
    in life.
Make us pleasant to all,
    But save us from all insincerity.

Help us, O God, to obey the great commandment of Jesus,
and to be perfect, as you, our Father in heaven, are perfect.

*A Prayer of Reinhold Niebuhr*

O God, give us,
    Serenity to accept what cannot be changed;
    Courage to change what should be changed;
    And wisdom to distinguish the one from the other:
        through Jesus Christ our Lord.   Amen.

*The Blessing*

The grace of the Lord Jesus Christ be with us all.   Amen.

*The Opening Prayer*

O God, our Father, for these few minutes fix our thoughts on you.

> Let no wandering thought distract our attention, and no impure thought keep us from listening.

Help us to worship you tonight with a concentrated attention and a clean heart: through Jesus Christ our Lord. Amen.

*The Reading Lesson:* II Timothy 2.1-7

*Prayer*

> Let us think of the titles by which the New
> Testament calls the Christians, that we may
> ask God's help to make them ours.

Jesus' men were called *disciples*, and *disciple* means a *learner*.

> O God, our Father, help us to be wise enough to know that we do not know; and so help us each day to store our minds with some new knowledge. Above all things, help us to know you better every day.

The Christians are called *brothers*.

> O God, help us in this place to be one united band of brothers. Grant that we may be able to argue and to differ without quarrelling, and grant that nothing may ever disturb our fellowship.

Jesus called his men his *friends*.

> O Lord Jesus, help us always to give you the loyalty and the fidelity which true friends ought to give, and help us to prove our friendship by doing what you command us to do.

Christians are to be *lights of the world*.

O God, help us to be a good example to all, that we may ever help them to walk in the right way, and never make it easier for them to go wrong.

Christians are to be *the salt of the earth*.

O God, just as salt gives flavour to things, and keeps things from being tasteless and insipid, help us so to live that we may make life thrilling for ourselves and for others.

Christians are to be good *soldiers*.

Help us, O God, to be always under discipline, always ready to obey the word of your command, always ready to go where you send us, always proud to show whose we are and whom we serve.

Jesus called his men *apostles*, and *apostle* means *ambassador*.

Lord Jesus, help us at all times to be your ambassadors, so that by our life and our example we may commend to others the faith which our lips profess.

Christians are to be *advertisements* for Jesus.

Lord Jesus, you meant us to be open letters for you, which every one can read; help us always to bring credit and honour, and never discredit and dishonour on the name we bear.

## *A Prayer of Charles Kingsley*

Guide us, teach us, and strengthen us, O Lord, we beseech thee, until we become such as thou wouldst have us to be; pure, gentle, truthful, high-minded, courteous, generous, able, dutiful and useful; for thy honour and glory. Amen.

## *The Blessing*

The blessing of God, the Father, the Son and the Holy Spirit, be on us, and stay with us all. Amen.

# TO BE USEFUL AND HELPFUL

*The Opening Prayer*

O God, our Father, we ask you tonight to
    Strengthen us where we are weak;
    Instruct us where we are ignorant;
    Correct us where we are in error;
    Make us stronger in that which we are already strong.

So grant that we may feel, when this act of worship is done, that it was good for us to have been here: through Jesus Christ our Lord.  Amen.

*The Reading Lesson:* Proverbs 22.1-12

*Prayer*

O God, our Father, make us the kind of people who are really useful and really helpful.

    Help us, when we are asked, to do with a good grace even that which we do not want to do, and that which no one else will do.

    Help us never to take offence, if someone else is asked to do what we thought we should have been asked to do.

    Help us never to think of praise and prestige, and credit and thanks, so long as the work is done.

    Help us to be equally willing to take the first place and to take the last place.

    Help us, when we are asked to do something, to be more ready to say yes and to say no.

    Help us willingly to use whatever talents you gave us in the service of others.

> Help us always to be volunteers and not conscripts when some job has to be done.
>
> Help us always to be willing to give up time and pleasure and leisure when someone is required to do some useful work.

Help us in all things to be like Jesus, amongst our fellowmen as they who serve.

## A Prayer of Archbishop Laud

Lord, here we are, do with us as seemeth best in thine own eyes, only give us, we humbly beseech thee, a penitent and a patient spirit to expect thee. Lord, make our service acceptable to thee while we live, and our souls ready for thee when we die: for the sake of Jesus Christ thy Son our Saviour. Amen.

## The Blessing

The grace of our Lord Jesus Christ, and the love of God, and the fellowship of the Holy Spirit be with us all, and be with all whom we love here and everywhere, and stay with each one of us and them this night and always. Amen.

# THE RIGHT KIND OF LISTENING

*The Opening Prayer*

O God, our Father, there are so many things within us which so often keep us from hearing your voice as we ought:

> The pride, which does not recognize its own need;
> The self-will, which wants no way but its own;
> The wilful blindness, which refuses to see what it does not wish to see;
> The wilful deafness, which refuses to hear what it does not wish to hear;
> The false independence, which resents advice;
> The foolishness, which thinks that it knows best.

Take from us everything that would keep us from hearing your voice tonight, and help us to listen, to understand and to obey: through Jesus Christ our Lord. Amen.


*The Reading Lesson:* James 2.14-26


*Prayer*

O God, a great deal of our life is spent listening to others, who teach us, and who tell us what we ought to do. We have to listen to parents, to teachers, to instructors, to preachers, to all who give us advice, guidance and sometimes rebuke. Help us always to listen in the right way.

> Help us to listen with attention,
> > not to let our thoughts wander, to concentrate on what we hear, that it may really stay in our minds, and not go into one ear and out of the other.

218

Help us to listen and to understand,
   Help us not to give up thinking, questioning, enquiring, until we really find what a thing means.

Help us to listen and to remember.
   Help us not to hear, and then go away and forget all about what we have heard. Give us minds which are interested, for only then can we have memories which are retentive.

Help us to listen and to act.
   Help us to put into practice that which we are taught, both at our day's work and at our instruction in the faith. Help us to remember always that words are poor things without deeds, and that faith without works is dead.

And so grant that hearing, understanding, remembering and doing may ever go hand in hand.

## A Jewish Prayer

O our Father, grant peace, happiness, and blessing, grace, favour, and mercy, unto all thy people. Bless us, even all of us together, with the light of thy countenance; for by the light of thy face thou hast given us, O Eternal God, the law of life, gracious love, righteousness, blessing, mercy, life, and peace. May it be pleasing in thy sight to bless thy people at all times, and at all seasons with thy peace: for thy Name's sake. Amen.

## The Blessing

Unto God's gracious mercy and protection we commit ourselves. The Lord bless us and keep us. The Lord make his face to shine upon us and be gracious unto us. The Lord lift up the light of his countenance upon us, and give us peace, both now and evermore. Amen.

# THE VISION OF PEACE

*The Opening Prayer*

O God, our Father,
 Increase our knowledge this night,
  that we may know more about you, and more about
   the life which you want us to live.
 Increase our strength of mind and our will-power,
  that we may be able better to keep the resolutions that
   we have made.
 Increase our love,
  that we may be ever more devoted to Jesus, and that,
   so loving him more, we may be more true to him,
   and serve him better.
This we ask for your love's sake.  Amen.

*The Reading Lesson:* Isaiah 11.1-9

> We have listened to the vision of the time,
> when no one shall hurt or destroy, and when
> all violence and hatred shall cease. Let us
> pray that we may be able to help to bring
> that time nearer.

*Prayer*

O God, our Father, you are the God of peace. Help us to
make peace.

 Help us to have peace in our relationships with others.
  Give us the forbearing and the forgiving spirit. Keep
  us from being quick to take offence. Control both our
  temper and our tongue. Help us not to be so quick to
  condemn what we do not understand, and, when

people think differently from us, help us to remember that they too have a right to their opinions, and help us always to treat others as we would have them treat us.

Help us to do all we can to bring peace among men. When we meet those of another race or of another colour, or of another party, or of another religion, help us to treat them as friends and not as strangers. Help us to see our nation's greatness, not in mastering other peoples, but in serving them, and in bringing them to a stage when they can take their full and independent place in the life and the work and the councils of the world, not in ruling others, but in helping them to rule themselves.

Help us to do all we can by our prayers, by our conduct, by our words, by our actions, by the giving of money, when money is needed, to bring quickly the day when everyone in the world will know you and love you, so that the day will come when all men will know that they are brothers because you are their one Father.

### A Prayer from the Mozarabic Liturgy

O God, who art peace everlasting, whose chosen reward is the gift of peace, and who hast taught us that the peace-makers are thy children, pour thy peace into our souls, that everything discordant may utterly vanish, and all that makes for peace be sweet to us for ever: through Jesus Christ our Lord.  Amen.

### The Blessing

The peace of God which passeth all understanding keep our hearts and minds in the knowledge and the love of God, and of his Son Jesus Christ our Lord, and the blessing of God Almighty, the Father, the Son, and the Holy Spirit, be amongst us and remain with us always.  Amen.

# WISDOM TO DECIDE ARIGHT

*The Opening Prayer*

O God, you can make all things new. Make us new tonight.
Cleanse our aims and desires,
that we may never set our hearts on any wrong thing.
Cleanse our impulses, our emotions and our ambitions,
that we may never be swept into any wrong action.
Cleanse our minds and our thoughts,
that they may never travel down any forbidden pathway or linger on any forbidden thing.
Cleanse our words and our speaking,
that we may utter no word which we would not wish you to hear.
And grant that being cleansed in heart and in mind, we may pray and think and speak more nearly as we ought: through Jesus Christ our Lord. Amen.

*The Reading Lesson:* Proverbs 17.1-10

*Prayer*

Give us, O God, the wisdom which will enable us at all times to know what to do.
Make us to know,
When to speak and when to be silent.
Grant that no cowardice may keep us from speaking when we ought to speak, and grant that no angry passion may make us speak, when we would regret having spoken.

Make us to know,
When to say No and when to say Yes.

Grant that no weakness may make us yield to, or agree with, that which is wrong, and grant that no self-will may make us unreasonably and stubbornly set on our own way.

Make us to know,
When to criticize and when to praise.
Grant that no too easy tolerance may make us unprotestingly accept that which is wrong, and that no ungracious discourtesy may keep us from speaking the word of encouragement which means so much.

Make us to know,
When to act and when to wait.
Help us to recognize the things which must be done at once, if they are to be done at all, and to see what things cannot be hurried and for which we must in patience wait.

*A Prayer of Anselm*

We bring before thee, O Lord, the troubles and perils of people and nations, the sighing of the prisoners and captives, the sorrows of the bereaved, the necessities of strangers, the helplessness of the weak, the despondency of the weary, the failing powers of the aged. O Lord, draw near to each: for the sake of Jesus Christ our Lord. Amen.

*The Blessing*

The grace of the Lord Jesus Christ be with us all. Amen.

# ACKNOWLEDGMENTS

Our grateful thanks are due to the Oxford University Press for the use of two prayers from *Daily Prayer* by E. Milner-White and G. W. Briggs; and one prayer from *A Diary of Private Prayer* by John Baillie; and to Peter Davies Ltd for permission to include a prayer from *Prayers* by Peter Marshall.